THE SPIRITUALITY
OF COMMUNITY

Catholic Spirituality for Adults

General Editor
Michael Leach

Other Books in the Series

Prayer by Joyce Rupp
Reconciliation by Robert Morneau
Holiness by William J. O'Malley
Diversity of Vocations by Marie Dennis
Eucharist by Robert Barron
Charity by Virgil Elizondo
Listening to God's Word by Alice Camille
Mary by Kathy Coffey

THE SPIRITUALITY
OF COMMUNITY

※

Adele J. Gonzalez

Maryknoll, New York 10545

Founded in 1970, Orbis Books endeavors to publish works that enlighten the mind, nourish the spirit, and challenge the conscience. The publishing arm of the Maryknoll Fathers and Brothers, Orbis seeks to explore the global dimensions of the Christian faith and mission, to invite dialogue with diverse cultures and religious traditions, and to serve the cause of reconciliation and peace. The books published reflect the views of their authors and do not represent the official position of the Maryknoll Society. To learn more about Maryknoll and Orbis Books, please visit our website at www.maryknollsociety.org.

Library of Congress Cataloging-in-Publication Data

Gonzalez, Adelaida J.
    The spirituality of community / Adele J. Gonzalez.
      p. cm. – (Catholic spirituality for adults)
    Includes bibliographical references and index.
    ISBN 978-1-57075-718-1 (pbk. : alk. paper)
    1. Christian communities – Catholic Church 2. Communities – Religious aspects – Catholic Church. 3. Fellowship – Religious aspects – Catholic Church. I. Title.
BX2347.7.G66 2009
248.4'82 – dc22
                                  2009007890

Contents

Introduction to Catholic Spirituality for Adults

C ATHOLIC SPIRITUALITY FOR ADULTS explores the deepest dimension of spirituality, that place in the soul where faith meets understanding. When we reach that place we begin to see as if for the first time. We are like the blind man in the Gospel who could not believe his eyes: "And now I see!"

Catholicism is about seeing the good of God that is in front of our eyes, within us, and all around us. It is about learning to see Christ Jesus with the eyes of Christ Jesus, the Way, the Truth, and the Life.

Only when we *see* who we are as brothers and sisters of Christ and children of God can we begin to *be* like Jesus and walk in his Way. "As you think in your heart, so you are" (Prov. 23:7).

Catholic Spirituality for Adults is for those of us who want to make real, here and now, the words we once learned in school. It is designed to help us go beyond information to transformation. "When I was a child, I spoke as a child, I understood as a child, I thought as a child, but when I became an adult, I put away childish things" (1 Cor. 13:11).

The contributors to the series are the best Catholic authors writing today. We have asked them to explore the deepest dimension of their own faith and to share with us what they are learning to see. Topics covered range from prayer — "Be still, and know that I am God" (Ps. 46:10) — to our purpose in life — coming to know "that God has given us eternal life, and this life is in his Son" (1 John 5:11) — to simply getting through the day — "Put on compassion, kindness, humility, gentleness, and patience" (Col. 3:12).

Each book in this series reflects Christ's active and loving presence in the world. The authors celebrate our membership in the mystical body of Christ, help us to understand our spiritual unity with the entire family of God, and encourage us to express Christ's mission of love, peace, and reconciliation in our daily lives.

Catholic Spirituality for Adults is the fruit of a publishing partnership between Orbis Books, the publishing arm of the Catholic Foreign Mission Society of America (Maryknoll), and RCL Benziger, a leading provider of religious and family life education for all ages. This series is rooted in vital Catholic traditions and committed to a continuing standard of excellence.

Michael Leach
General Editor

Acknowledgments

My deepest gratitude to

Michael Leach, my editor, for his wisdom,
guidance, and understanding

All the wonderful Christians, fellow sojourners,
who so openly and unreservedly
enrich my work and my life
with their stories of faith

Author's Introduction:
An Ordinary Catholic

IF I COULD PARAPHRASE SCRIPTURE to reflect my years in pastoral ministry, the Gospel according to St. Matthew, chapter 18, verse 20, would read differently. Jesus' promise, "Where two or three are gathered together in my name, there am I in the midst of them," would change to, "Where two or three are gathered together in my name...challenges emerge, thus *I have* to be in their midst!"

I have shared this idea with many Christians who claim that I am being negative, that when Christians gather to pray and grow together wonderful things happen. I am amazed that the joy of community living was not the first thought that came to me when I began to plan for this book. The notion of the community of the disciples, of one heart and one mind, beloved of God and bound together in loving service took longer to emerge in my consciousness. And yet I belong to a small Christian community, to a parish community, and to the global community. Am I a hypocrite? Am I helping to foster something in which I do not believe?

Actually, I am an optimist and a woman of hope, and these gifts enable me to look at challenges and conflict in community life in truth without fear. As we will later see, conflict can be a positive force for growth, one that from the early days of the first Christian communities helped to shape and form the new believers and to open the doors for the expansion of their faith.

Another concept that arose about spirituality is as surprising as the first. Hundreds of inspirational books have been written about Christian spirituality and about community. They tell about extraordinary experiences of the Spirit transforming small groups of Christians and inspiring them to be the leaven that can transform the world. But do we need another book like those? While I do not bring any new theological insight to the topic, I believe that I am looking at it from a different perspective, which I share with the average lay Catholic adult in the church today.

While I am a pastoral minister, a spiritual companion, I am also one of the people in the pews that I minister to and with. Many of the books in the market today target a sophisticated readership: clergy, religious, and people who are in professional ministry. This book is directed to those of us who are totally immersed in the world and who desperately need to find God in the midst of our everyday life.

For years I have heard comments such as these: "I went to a conference [or retreat], which was very good. I bought all the books they were selling, but to be honest I have not read any. I seldom have the time or the space to read such deep writings." More recently, books have been written for the average Catholic. They are excellent but tend to content themselves with "prayers" or instructions on how to pray. People who enjoy reading them certainly grow in their prayer practice, but not necessarily in their understanding of Christian spirituality and even less of the spirituality of community, given that such books are primarily devotional.

Moreover, because my ministry has always taken place in culturally diverse environments, I write this book to speak to people of different cultures, races, and socioeconomic backgrounds, but most of all, to the average Catholic in the pew or maybe "outside the pew." I bring to the conversation their collective wisdom as Catholics struggling to find God in the joy and the mess of their lives, hoping to be inspired by the Sunday Eucharist and, most of all, wanting to belong to the community of the beloved disciples, even when their experience falls short of their expectations.

It is my hope and prayer that many Catholic adults will find these ideas insightful, refreshing, and energizing as they try to respond to the presence of the Spirit of our passionate God in our lives, our church, and our world, no matter what the challenges. God is truly with us.

Christian Spirituality

S PIRITUALITY IS ONE OF the most misunderstood
terms in Christianity. Many Catholics complain
that they do not find "spirituality" in their religion.
Fallen away or nonpracticing Catholics argue that
they are spiritual but do not go to church anymore.
They look for the spiritual in Zen practices, Yoga,
Eastern mysticism, and meditation, usually in non-
denominational groups, because they feel empty in
their familiar Catholic tradition. The celebration of
the Eucharist does not satisfy them if the priest is
not a good preacher or the choir does not excel,
and in many cases, traditional devotions have lost
the meaning and relevancy they once had.

On the other side of the spectrum, many devotional practices such as the Divine Mercy Chaplet
and new Marian devotions are spreading rapidly, and
there is a rebirth in the tradition of spending time
in adoration before the Blessed Sacrament. Yet for
many lay adults today, the term "Catholic spirituality" is an oxymoron. Many believe that Catholic

basically means following rules, believing dogmas, and making sure that one has "acquired" all the necessary sacraments for salvation, but that it has nothing to do with being spiritual. Often, these two extremes appear to be at odds with each other. In the derogatory parlance that I sometimes hear, there are "those New Age" Catholics on one side and "those pre-Vatican pious" Catholics on the other. In the midst of this wrestling match, the true meaning of Christian spirituality gets lost.

To add to the confusion, some people use the term "spiritual" to refer to external appearances, persons who "look spiritual." If asked what they mean by that, they describe someone who is quiet and at times even boring. Those who look at spirituality this way usually feel less spiritual than the person they are talking about. "I am not like her" is a frequent remark I hear; "she is so good, so holy."

Without diminishing the quality of anyone's spiritual life, it appears that for many Catholics today, spirituality and an overt pious life are one and the same. It is not surprising then to find spirituality identified with piety and devotional practices. These are indeed an integral part of one's relationship with God, but spirituality goes deeper than religious disciplines and external appearances. The purpose of this chapter is to bring a fresh understanding to the topic, one to which readers in parishes, colleges, and formation programs can relate.

᠅

The word "spirituality" does not belong to one religion. We can speak of a Hindu spirituality, a Jewish spirituality, a Muslim spirituality, a Buddhist spirituality, etc. When we refer to Christian spirituality we mean our lives with the Spirit, the way in which we relate and respond to the presence of the Spirit of God in our lives. It is our life with the Spirit (Gal. 5:25).

The word "spirituality" is not used to measure levels, as if we were talking about temperature or humidity. Spirituality is not quantified in degrees; rather, spirituality is our response to God revealed moment by moment. Because, as we said before, Christian spirituality is our life with the Spirit, it implies relationships, *all* relationships. As human beings we live out our spirituality in the world through four relationships:

1. God (Transcendent)

When we refer to God as transcendent we mean that God is more than any image of God we could have.

Whether I see God as Father, spouse, mother, Savior, friend, etc., God is beyond all these concepts put together. The quality of transcendence also implies that I am not God.

Some religious traditions do not make a distinction between the self and a god. For Christians, God is the One, the Ground of our being, the reason for our existence, the Creator, the Sustainer. In Catholicism we have a long history of people (mystics) who seek union with the transcendent God — a God totally "other." God transcends the universe, but also transcends knowledge; God is beyond the grasp of the human mind.

Christians believe that God is both within and beyond the universe, capable of being found in everything and everyone and yet surpassing everything and everyone.

When I look at a newborn baby, I see a masterpiece, the work of a great artist, but the biological parents are not the artist. In that baby, I see the handiwork of the Supreme Artist, of God who is Love and transcends me, the baby, and the parents.

2. Myself (God Within)

St. Francis of Assisi often prayed with a simple question, "Who am I God, and who are you?" He knew that God and the human person are in intimate communion, and that it is important to know who is who. If God is my Creator, and I have been created in God's image and likeness, then there is a spark of the Divine in me. As a Christian I do believe that I am the temple of God's Spirit and that the Spirit dwells within each one of us. This quality is known as immanence, and it is often defined as the opposite of transcendence; the two are not mutually exclusive. Christians believe that God is both within and beyond the universe, capable of being found in everything and everyone and yet surpassing everything and everyone. A transcendent God is one who is wholly "other" when compared to us. An immanent God is one who exists within us and within the universe, very much a part of our existence. The fact that transcendence and immanence exist simultaneously is part of what we call "the Mystery of God."

When Isaiah the prophet wrote about the Messiah, he said, "The Lord himself will give you a sign. Look, the young woman is with child and shall bear a son, and shall name him Immanuel," meaning God is with us (Isa. 7:14). Since ancient times, Jews knew

that God was always with them, guiding and pro-
tecting the people. We Christians believe that over
two thousand years ago, the Word of God became
flesh in Jesus Christ, the Immanuel. Because of creation and of the Incarnation we affirm that God is
with us and within us while remaining beyond our
total grasp.

St. Paul proclaimed in the city of Athens: "He
[God] made all nations to inhabit the whole earth . . .
so that they would search for God . . . though indeed
he is not far from each one of us. For 'in him we live
and move and have our being' " (Acts 17:26–28).

This life in God calls me to develop a healthy
relationship with myself.

If I live and move and have my being in Christ,
addictions of any kind — drugs, alcohol, work, gam-
bling, sex — hurt me as a person and, therefore,
my relationship with God. There are other subtle
ways to do this: greed, violent behavior, inability
to forgive, holding grudges, regretting the past, and
anxiously anticipating the future while missing the
present. Some of us are unable to believe that God
loves us, unable to forgive ourselves and even less to
love ourselves. It is sad when this happens, because
this forgiveness and love are the foundations of our
relationship with ourselves.

3. My Neighbor (God Immanently Present)

The concept of immanence also applies here. If God's Spirit lives in me, then God also lives in the people around me. I cannot claim to have a healthy relationship with God and myself if I ignore those around me. Traditionally the word "neighbor" meant the person who lived in my neighborhood or on my block. Jesus extended the meaning of the word to include anyone who helps a person in need. By neighbor, I mean any human being who shares planet earth with me. We are all bound together by an invisible bond that extends beyond geographical barriers or political ideologies. "Your love for God is only as great as the love you have for the person you love the least" (Dorothy Day).

The following text taken from the Letter of Paul to the Romans summarizes the nature of the relationship we are called to have with our neighbor:

Let love be genuine; hate what is evil, hold fast to what is good; love one another with mutual affection; outdo one another in showing honor. ...Contribute to the needs of the saints; extend hospitality to strangers. Bless those who persecute you; bless and do not curse them. Rejoice with those who rejoice, weep with those who weep. Live in harmony with one another; do not be haughty, but associate with the lowly; do not claim to be wiser than you are. Do not repay anyone evil for evil, but take thought for what is noble in the sight of all. If it is possible, so far as it depends on you, live peaceably with all. Beloved, never avenge yourselves, but leave room for the wrath of God; for it is written, "Vengeance is mine, I will repay, says the Lord." No, "if your enemies are hungry, feed them; if they are thirsty, give them something to drink; for by doing this you will heap burning coals on their heads. Do not be overcome by evil, but overcome evil with good." (Rom. 12:9–21)

4. All Creation

Creation can be defined in a variety of ways. To me, creation is a gift from God, the loving Source of all that is. I have placed a tremendous importance on the relationships with self and others, this is because the "human spiritual project is carried out in the context of other human persons and the world of nature."[1] I believe that creation is good and that God is faithful and, therefore, both human beings and the world can be healed. Today many people look at the world with an apocalyptic fear of its coming to an end through a final catastrophic destruction. I see creation moving to its final fulfillment, through a transformation of love, but I also believe that God will not interfere with the free actions of some people who choose a negative route toward creation's final end.

This fourth and last relationship of Christian spirituality is often ignored. But we need to become aware that it is in the world where our spiritual journey is to be lived. To be a Christian is not a way to escape this world, but a life in and with God in the world.

⁂

Because we are always in relationships, we live out our spirituality in our family life, profession, leisure time, ministry, and prayer.

What happens then when we describe ourselves as nonspiritual or as less spiritual than someone else? What do we measure? Who or what do we hold up as the ideal or the norm for the spiritual person?

First of all, there is a spiritual inferiority complex rooted in the fourth century, when spirituality became the exclusive "gift" of monasticism or eremitical life. Ordinary Christians went to the desert or monasteries looking for the wisdom of these fathers and mothers that had devoted their lives to prayer and the knowledge of God. The strong asceticism of these men and women reinforced the notion that "worldly" concerns were an obstacle to spiritual development.

As time went by, those Christians who stayed in the cities and lived an ordinary life began to see themselves as incapable of reaching the spiritual "heights" of the "holy ones."

One of the elements of the Greek culture in which Christianity emerged was dualism. In the field of spirituality dualism meant that the body and the spirit were two opposite realities. For a person to be considered spiritual, he or she had to reject material things, including especially the body. Most of us were brought up assuming that this dualism was central to the Christian experience.

If people were given the freedom to express their experiences of God, without any expectation that they use a specific vocabulary, most would be surprised at the depth and richness of their own religious experiences.

We are spiritual because the Holy Spirit of God dwells within us, not because we try to avoid or even reject all material reality. A very good friend and I have been spiritual companions for many years. Although she is up to date in theological developments, she has the habit of calling me "Great Guru." Although we both take it as a joke, the name carries the covert understanding that I am holier than she because I have been a pastoral minister in the church for so many years.

Obviously, Christians who devote all their energies to their spiritual growth may well develop a richer prayer life. The mistake is to believe that they are somehow superior to other Christians and that the ordinary lay person does not have the capacity for contemplation or for the deep encounter with God available only in monasteries or religious orders.

I am convinced that if people were given the freedom to express their experiences of God, without any expectation that they use a specific vocabulary, most would be surprised at the depth and richness of their own religious experiences.

In a recent retreat, a young woman from the Dominican Republic shared with great passion her experience of God as merciful and compassionate, a true friend. She said she found God in everything, especially in her students, and also in every situation of her life, even the painful and messy ones. As she continued to talk about God as "He," she suddenly began to tell us about her mother. She described her with all the attributes that she had previously used to describe God. "My mother is great," she said, "she is my friend, very understanding and compassionate." After a few more stories about her mother she exclaimed, "God has always been 'Father' to me, and I am not a feminist. Yet something within is telling me also to consider God as a Mother. I cannot say anymore at this point."

This young woman's story illustrates how traditional understandings can influence one's image of God to the point of denying our true religious experiences. In her native country, she grew up with the image of *Papá* Dios. All the retreats she ever attended were directed by men, mostly priests, and the spiritual jargon was filled with masculine terms. In the United States, she was turned off by what she understood as feminism. Nevertheless, at this point in her spiritual journey, she was experiencing a maternal side of God that she was unable to own. She thought she was offending God by using feminine terms, and at the same time she rejected any opening to the feminine for fear of falling into "radical feminism."

Another woman from Haiti, who works as a social worker with AIDS victims, was not able to conceptualize her experience or image of God. Rather, she described it. "I find God in moments like this, with a group of good friends sharing about our lives. God is here. I also find God in the children sick with AIDS. God is everywhere and in everything." In this woman's life there was no dualism between sacred and profane, good and bad; she saw God in joy and in suffering, in health and in illness, in churches and in hospitals. "It is all part of living, and God is in all life," she concluded.

Her spirituality is earthy, similar to that of Francis of Assisi. She has befriended her joys and her sadness, her losses and her gains. Her life is totally committed to alleviating the suffering of others. Yet she did not consider herself a "spiritual person," just a simple servant. To her, spiritual people were more detached from the world, not as involved as she was. They certainly spent more time praying or in devotional practices.

If she had not been offered this opportunity to speak her truth in her own words, without fear of being ridiculed, we would have never known the depth and breadth of her spirituality.

We need to liberate spirituality from the notion that it means living as otherworldly, flawlessly perfect eccentrics. We also need a "liberating spirituality" that will help discover and affirm the voices of the simple, ordinary Christians whose stories and spiritual journeys are not recorded in our history books.

Our Catholic tradition is rich with stories of faith. We are a people of stories, and we are tellers of the One Story, the Incarnation of the God of Love and

God's total immersion in everything human, especially suffering and pain. How this Story is lived and experienced is profoundly influenced by our context. It is precisely our Christian faith that tells me that our spirituality does not fall from the sky, but rather it is deeply rooted in the mystery of the Incarnation, and therefore it happens here and now.

One of these colorful stories is the life of Dorothy Day, born in Brooklyn, New York, in 1897. Dorothy lived in the midst of social and political turmoil. Hers were times of fear of Communism and of any political position that would reflect it. Dorothy began her career in groups of intellectual protestors and troublemakers. After a conversion experience she became a Catholic and was known as a social activist, a journalist, a pacifist, and a founder of the Catholic Worker movement in 1933. At first the Catholic Worker was only a newspaper, but eventually it became a house of hospitality for the poor and the homeless. By 1936 there were thirty-three Catholic Worker houses across the country.

One of the miracles of Dorothy's life is that she remained part of a conflict-torn community for nearly half a century. Yet she always remained a person of hope and gratitude. Dorothy had a strong and difficult personality and was known for losing her temper. These seemed like negative Christian attributes, and yet these were the qualities that God used to make her the advocate of the poor and the homeless of her time.

If society and church had not been able to hear her unconventional voice, we would be the poorer for it. She enriched Christian spirituality with a radical commitment to the poor seldom found in a stubborn lay woman in the twentieth century. Dorothy's ministry took place in a community setting, and many viewed this community as a blessed place of love. A member of the community once said:

> People sometimes tell me how lucky I am to have been part of the same community that Dorothy Day belonged to. They picture a group of more or less saintly people having a wonderful time doing good works. In reality Catholic Worker community life in Manhattan in the early sixties had much in common with purgatory. The "staff" was made up of people with very different backgrounds, interests, temperaments, and convictions. Agreement within the staff was as rare as visits by the president of the United States....
>
> Though we worked side by side, saw each other daily, and prayed together, staff tension had become too acute for staff meetings.[2]

What got her into the most trouble was her pacifist stance. Dorothy believed that a nonviolent way
of life was at the heart of the Gospel. Many regarded
Dorothy as a saint, something she never liked. Her
response on one of these occasions says it all: "Don't
call me a saint. I don't want to be dismissed so
easily."

---

*When nothing was happening I
wondered if God was really with
me. In the meantime God was all
around, but I could not see him.*

Dorothy confuses many Christians today. Should
she be canonized? How about her many "sins,"
including abortion? What kind of a saint was she?
Although she defied all the conventional definitions
of a saint, her life and message have been one of
the leading lights of twentieth-century spirituality,
and her story remains an important part of the
Christian story.

⁕|⁕

As part of my ministry, I work with small Christian
communities, and I also belong to two of them. Some
of the stories that I have heard through the years
illustrate the difficulties that lay people encounter

when their voices do not find a sacred space to share their experiences of God.

During the gathering of one of these groups made up of people from different cultural backgrounds, one young man exclaimed, "God is playing hide-and-seek with me. I have tried to be faithful; I go to Mass daily and read the Bible, but I am exhausted from chasing God." His comments were followed by the silence that usually reflects either the depth of an insight or the bewilderment of the listeners. I think in this case there was a little of both. Perhaps he was focusing too narrowly on God's presence in his life.

In another occasion, a middle-aged physician complained of dryness in his prayer. "I am in a desert," he said. "This is a very depressing time for me." I asked if he could elaborate more on his experience, and he continued, "I am reading the Bible every day and praying the Liturgy of the Hours, but I cannot find God." Someone asked him if there was any place where he sensed the presence of the Divine. He quickly responded, "I see God in my patients everyday, especially the elderly. When they tell me about their pain and suffering I feel great compassion and I know that God is there in my compassion and in their pain. It is very moving." After a pause, I said, "Perhaps you are determined to find God 'your way' while all along God is trying to reveal God's presence differently." After a long pause, he said, "When nothing was happening I wondered if God was really with me. In the meantime God was all around, but I could not see him."

These stories represent my experience of many years as a spiritual companion and lay minister in the Roman Catholic tradition: many lay women and men, regardless of their cultural backgrounds, are frustrated because they feel unable to experience God in their daily lives. They try hard to find God in predetermined ways and places while often ignoring the *Immanuel, God-with-us,* already present in their midst waiting to be discovered. Today, more than ever, we are all called to become for one another seers of God's presence and activity in our here and now.

In the next chapter, I explore three characteristics of Christian spirituality that contribute to the understanding of this elusive term. Christian spirituality is by its very nature *passionate, communal,* and *contextual,* because it is rooted in the Incarnation:

- *Passionate* because God is love and has an everlasting desire for us;

- *Communal* because we are a people; Christianity is a communal faith;

- *Contextual* because it is incarnate, rooted in the here and now.

Christian faith believes that Jesus of Nazareth is the Word of God made flesh. In Jesus God's desire to freely communicate with us achieved a concrete historical manifestation. Jesus is more than a great prophet or the awaited Jewish Messiah. Christians believe that in Jesus, the Creator God dramatically entered our history and is affected by what we do to one another (see Matt. 25:31–46; John 14:8–9; Phil. 2:5–8). Christians believe that human beings are created in the image and likeness of God with a desire and longing for divinity. In the Incarnation the Divine became human, embracing all of humanity so that the human could become divine. This intimate communion between Creator and creation, Lover and beloved, has radical implications for Christian spirituality.

The Mystery of the Incarnation

What exactly is the meaning of the Incarnation, the belief that the Word of God became flesh in Jesus the Christ over two thousand years ago?

Usually the celebration of this feast is limited to Christmas. Jesus is born as a human baby in a manger. The Christmas story is probably the most beautiful story ever told. Why then do we spend the Advent season shopping? Why is Santa Claus almost as important as Jesus in some families? Why do we put up decorations right after Thanksgiving and take them down on December 26? Do we not know that Christmas lasts until the Feast of the Epiphany, the visit of the Magi to the manger?

In my experience it is not a good idea to plan any parish activity after December 10. Past that unspoken deadline we know that no one will attend because everyone is involved in shopping or cooking for Christmas. Why are we so hesitant to see Christmas as the great Feast of the Incarnation, of the Word of God made flesh, of the Divine penetrating the human? History has played a part in this lack of understanding.

The most common way of looking at the coming of the Immanuel, God-with-us, emphasizes redemption. It goes back to original sin as the fundamental alienation from God, a separation so profound that only God could "fix it." Traditionally, the Incarnation has been explained as God's action to right our original wrong, and this is the most common definition even today. The purpose of Jesus' life is linked to original sin and human sinfulness. Thus, without sin, there would have been no need for the Incarnation.[3]

This approach demonstrates God's unconditional love in his willingness to forgive us and offer us salvation. This is a valid but limited position that does not do justice to the awesomeness of the Incarnation.

There are other ways of understanding the Incarnation that are orthodox and valid in our Catholic tradition and more helpful to our understanding and appreciating the love of God that is with us always. Perhaps the most important proponent of a richer understanding of the Incarnation was Franciscan theologian and philosopher John Duns Scotus (c. 1265–1308). His belief in the Incarnation was based on the central role of Christ in the universe and is firmly rooted in the Franciscan intellectual and spiritual tradition, at whose core is the Person of the Incarnate Son.

According to Scotus, the Incarnation was not a contingency plan put into effect when God's original creation project failed because of sin. Scotus rejected this notion because it implies that God's act of love was determined by an external necessity, i.e., redemption from sin.

Scotus understands the Incarnation as always being in the mind of God even before the historical and existential physicality of creation itself and the fact of sin. The Incarnation is the model for creation: there is a creation only because of the Incarnation. In this schema, the universe is for Christ and not Christ for the universe. Scotus finds it inconceivable that the "greatest good in the universe" i.e., the Incarnation, can be determined by some lesser good, i.e., man's redemption. This is because such a sin-centered view of the Incarnation suggests that the primary role of Christ is as an assuager of the universe's guilt. In the Absolute Primacy, Christ is the beginning, middle, and end of creation. He stands at the center of the universe as the reason for its existence.[4]

Scotus's position is in total accord with some of the central Christological statements of the New Testament.

The Prologue of the Gospel according to John states, "In the beginning was the Word, and the Word was with God, and the Word was God. He was in the beginning with God. All things came to be through him, and without him nothing came to be. What came to be through him was life, and this life was the light of the human race" (John 1:1–4). There is nothing in these statements that speaks of Christ as an afterthought provoked by the Fall. "For the Son of God became man so that we might become God. The only-begotten Son of God, wanting to make us sharers in his divinity, assumed our nature, so that he, made man, might make men gods."[5] The Son of God did not become incarnate only to save us from our sins but as the fulfillment of creation and of the fullness of God's desire to be-with-us. We could claim that the purpose of Jesus' life is the fulfillment of God's eternal longing to become one with us.

By 90 C.E. most of the New Testament Letters had been written, reflecting the beliefs and practices of the early church. In the Christological hymn that appears in the Letter of Paul to the Colossians, Christ is praised as the icon or image of the invisible God: he manifests God's presence in his person. Christ is called the firstborn of all creation because everything else was created through his mediation. Moreover, Paul clearly affirms that "all things were created through him and for him. He is before all things, and in him all things hold together" (1:16–17). Christ is preeminent and supreme as God's agent in the creation of all things, as prior to all things, sin included.

The last example is another Christological hymn, found in Paul's Letter to the Ephesians: "God has given us the wisdom to understand fully the mystery, the plan he was pleased to decree in Christ, to be carried out in the fullness of time: namely, to bring all things in the heavens and on earth into one under Christ's leadership" (1:9–10).

÷|÷

In my ministry and in my own spiritual journey, I am always mindful of the fruits of religious experiences. When I feel a certain pride after delivering an inspired speech, I say to myself, "So what?" What are the fruits of this gift God has given me? Am I more tolerant and forgiving? less critical? more accepting? These questions help me evaluate the quality of my relationship with God, especially when I begin to boast.

I have been very clear about my belief in the Mystery of the Incarnation. I talk and write about it. I teach it in my classes. "What's the big deal?" one could ask. I respond quoting the words of Gerard Manley Hopkins, S.J.: "My life is determined by the Incarnation down to most of the details of the day."

In very simple words, the Incarnation is what gives meaning to my life and provides the strength to keep on keeping on. I believe that the Creator of the cosmos is the principle of Love and an energy that never dies. This is a truth that sustains me. Creation was not an accident, and in whichever way if happened,

God was there. I believe that the source of all being is Love, and that we come from Love, live in Love, and are journeying toward a total fulfillment in Love. Obviously, these words are somewhat ethereal and do not seem to say anything concrete. To me they become fully real and expressed in the Mystery of the Incarnation. The Incarnation is more than a historical birth that took place over two thousand years ago. The Word of God takes flesh every day, not only on Christmas. This is the guiding light of my life. God spoke creation, has spoken all humanity, and finally this Word took flesh and became a human being.

This belief gives me a purpose. I do not know how many galaxies there are in the cosmos, or how long our planet will sustain human life. But I know that because there is a Spirit of Love charting the course and becoming flesh everyday, there is nothing to fear.

My total trust in the words of St. John the Evangelist, "God is love" (1 John 4:16), saves me from joining the prophets of doom who seem to multiply in our world today. If the universe was created by Love, in Love, and for Love, those apocalyptic battles of destruction make no sense. The fear that kidnaps so many people is contrary to the notion of a universe moving toward a transformation in Love. I live my life convinced that God desires me more than I desire God, and that my dreams of love, peace, unity, justice, and harmony are just reflections of God's Big Dream for the entire cosmos. I am more afraid of what we can do to the planet than of what God's plans for destruction may be.

I believe that God chose to embrace my humanity and this gives me permission to feel sadness, gratitude, wonderment, anguish, abandonment, despair, anger, joy, desire — everything that Jesus, the Word made flesh, experienced. The God I believe in is always here and now in ways that I cannot understand, and even less explain. But because of this belief, I know that I live, and move, and have my being in God. There is nothing to fear.

My belief in the Incarnation tells me, "God is right here, in the hospital bed, in the funeral home, unemployed, having open heart surgery."

Whether we are believers or not, when we read the Gospels, the humanity of the protagonist stands out. Jesus ate, slept, got tired, cried, needed the company of his friends, and suffered horrible tortures. In other words, he got fully immersed in the mess of humanity. When I hear people say, "Where was God when I needed him," I understand their pain and usually just listen. But my belief in the Incarnation tells me, "God is right here, in the hospital bed, in the funeral home, unemployed, having open heart surgery." Because of the Incarnation, there is no place where God is not. Thus in my mess it gives me great joy to know that God and I are playing in the same sandbox. God became human and by doing so made me divine. There is nothing to fear, or covet, or kill for.

This may sound strange to some, but the sandbox in which God and I play is filled with dirt and junk; it is not an orderly and immaculate sandbox, but it is not a chamber of horrors either. There are no snakes or boogie men in my mess, because they cannot coexist with the gentle power of God.

Life is painful, hard, and totally incomprehensible, but at the end of the day, I can look around and imagine God saying, "Let us make humankind in our image, according to our likeness; and when God saw everything that he had made, it was very good" (Gen. 1:26, 31). To me this is the attitude of a God who made the entire universe to be divine and then divinized it by becoming flesh. "For the Son of God became man so that we might become God."[6] There is nothing to fear.

A few years ago I directed a retreat called "Finding God in My Anger." During the retreat, I received a

letter from a priest telling me that I was wrong: God
cannot be found in anger, because anger was a capital
sin. I tried to answer the best I knew how and went
on with the retreat. If God is not present in my anger,
how was it possible for Jesus, the Word made flesh,
to be angry?

> Again he entered the synagogue, and a man was
> there who had a withered hand. They watched
> him to see whether he would cure him on the
> Sabbath, so that they might accuse him. And
> he said to the man who had the withered hand,
> "Come forward." Then he said to them, "Is it
> lawful to do good or to do harm on the Sab-
> bath, to save life or to kill?" But they were silent.
> He looked around at them **with anger**; he was
> grieved at their hardness of heart and said to the
> man, "Stretch out your hand." He stretched it
> out, and his hand was restored. (Mark 3:1–5)

Jesus' anger, just anger, resulted in an act of healing. An act of destruction, revenge, or hatred would
have turned the anger into violence.

We find good food for thought in the Letter to
the Ephesians: "Be angry but do not sin; do not let
the sun go down on your anger" (4:26). Is this not a
contradiction? Be angry but do not sin? If angry, seek
reconciliation that day or as soon as possible. Do

not let darkness turn your angry feelings into violent actions that could hurt you or others. Do not become possessed and controlled by your anger. You can turn the energy of anger into healing or forgiveness.

I find God in the dark places within me and in the world today, because I am convinced that "even the darkness is not dark to God; the night is as bright as the day, for darkness is as light to God" (Ps. 139:12).

I try to live the Christmas message of peace and love constantly, because Christmas goes on and on. Every day is Christmas, because every day God is with us. If you are reading this book and think, "I have never met anyone so out of touch with reality," I have news for you. I have been playing in the sandbox since I was a child. My father died suddenly when I was thirteen years old; my mother became blind. My brother and I had to flee Cuba because of the Communist regime. We came alone and lived in camps created by the Catholic Church to offer refuge to children. We were on our own for four years, and when our family finally came to the United States, they had become four elderly sick women who could not speak English or manage in this country. I am not a healthy person. I was diagnosed with rheumatoid arthritis at age thirty-five ... and I could go on and on, but this book is not about me; it is about the power of the Incarnation in the life of an ordinary person.

Last week I directed a retreat in a parish that had just lost one of its most beloved members to cancer. I knew the woman very well and spoke to her every week. The retreat was supposed to be about Advent and Christmas, but some were so sad that they could not even sing a Christmas carol. I understood their pain, because it was also mine, but I heard myself say, "We will never be truly Christians until we embrace sister death as part of life." Death is not the enemy, but one of the most beautiful gifts of the Incarnation. Our Creator chose to become a helpless baby like us, so that he could die a helpless death, also like us. There is nothing to fear.

> For I am convinced that neither death, nor life, nor angels, nor rulers, nor things present, nor things to come, nor powers, nor height, nor depth, nor anything else in all creation, will be able to separate us from the love of God in Christ Jesus our Lord. (Rom. 8:38–39)

Passionate, Communal, and Contextual

Passionate

ONE OF THE SADDEST FEELINGS a person can have is feeling unloved. We all thirst for love, longing to be in communion with someone in a meaningful relationship. Many of us are familiar with St. Augustine's comment in his *Confessions:* "Thou hast made us for thyself, O God, and our souls are restless till they find their rest in Thee." It is at least true to say that our souls are restless until we find our home somewhere, in something that feels adequate to our yearnings. The desire to love and to be loved is the fundamental gift of creation: "we are the image and likeness of the Lover."

This longing for love and intimacy enables us to relate not only to each other, but to God. Many spiritual writers claim that because this need for love can never be fully satisfied, we are forever "displacing" our longing. We look for fulfillment in wealth, power, control, possessions, and status. But the worst situation is when we try to find all of our fulfillment in relationships.

We place such a burden on each other: we want our spouses to "make us happy." We want our children to grow up to be the persons we want them to be. We want our parents to die without suffering and with a clear mind. When all these unrealistic expectations are not met, our fundamental desire for "divine love" is frustrated; we blame each other and destroy our relationships. We all know people who go through life unhappy simply because they refuse to accept that nothing and no one except God will ever satisfy them completely.

John the Evangelist defined God in an unambiguous way: "God is love" (1 John 4:16). This is one of the most important statements found in the Christian Scriptures. John speaks not of what God does, but of who God *is*. God is creator, father, mother, spouse, strength, cause, knowledge, and wisdom, but above all, God is Lover, and that means relational. The love of God is expressed in many ways, and it is always a source of wonderment for those who know how to see.

Have you ever looked at a sunset or at its rays breaking through the clouds and not wondered who is the Source of all this beauty? Can you witness a moment of birth and not marvel at the miracle of life? Have you ever experienced being forgiven and known the freedom of God's love? Creation, life itself, is one of the greatest acts of love that we can enjoy. But communicating God's self through creation was not enough. From the beginning God tried to enter into communion with all creatures. In the Old Testament God did so through events and the prophets. Time after time, God called the prophets to speak in God's name, and to convey his deep desire for union and intimacy with creation.

The words of God through the prophet Hosea declare that love:

> "I will allure her; I will lead her into the desert and speak to her heart." (2:13)

> "When Israel was a child I loved him.... The more I called them, the farther they went from me.... Yet it was I who took them in my arms; I drew them with human cords, with bands of love; I fostered them like one who raises an infant to his cheeks; Yet, though I stooped to feed my child, they did not know that I was their healer." (11:1–4)

These are not cold or tentative words. These declarations are full of passionate love. The relationship between the Lover (God) and God's people (the beloved) is magnificently portrayed in the Song of Songs, meaning the "greatest of songs," which contains in exquisite poetic form the sublime portrayal of the mutual love of God and his people:

> My lover speaks; he says to me, "Arise, my beloved, my beautiful one, and come! For see, the winter is past, the rains are over and gone. The flowers appear on the earth, the time of pruning the vines has come, and the song of the dove is heard in our land. The fig tree puts forth its figs, and the vines, in bloom, give forth fragrance. Arise, my beloved, my beautiful one, and come!" (2:10–13)

The words of this poem speak of love, passion, intimacy, desire. This is one of the ways in which the Bible attempts to capture God's relationship with us. But the Divine Lover was not satisfied with the childish response of a world unwilling or unable to grow and develop its full potential, a world that would not open up and accept God's offer of total communion. Thus, our faith tells us that, in the fullness of time, God became one with humanity in Jesus Christ, in whom the fullness of the Divine is revealed.

If God's creation and Incarnation are not enough to convince us of the relational nature of God, maybe the third aspect of God's self-revelation will. God's ultimate act of love is the indwelling of the Holy Spirit, who remains with us always. "Whoever loves me," Jesus said, "will keep my word, and my Father will love him, and we will come to him and make our dwelling with him" (John 14:23). The Creator God, and Jesus, the Word made flesh, would come together as Spirit to dwell forever in the human heart.

Each of us experiences this presence in different ways. Some describe it as a "knowing" that directs them and that they are sure comes from God. Others experience this indwelling through a sense of peace after making a difficult decision. For me personally it is more intuition than feeling. There is a presence, a force, an energy that moves me in one direction or another, and I know it is the Spirit guiding me here and now because there is peace and a sense of being in sync with God. This intuition usually comes when I am in silent meditation, letting my silence listen to God's silence. I also feel this presence when I am praying with Scriptures, reading, writing, taking pictures, experiencing nature, or playing with children.

The Apostle Paul clearly told the Christians in Corinth, "Do you not know that you are the temple of God, and that the Spirit of God dwells in you?" (1 Cor. 3:16). By the power of the Holy Spirit, God continues to be present to us, seeking everlasting communion with all creatures. This story of the Lover seeking the Beloved provides the foundation of the Christian concept of the Triune God. The Christian God is not a distant deity up there among the clouds but a God who desires an intimate communion with us through Jesus Christ in the Holy Spirit, a God who is relational, breaks through history, loves passionately, and becomes flesh in order to transform humanity.

Communal

It has been said that to be human is to be on a journey, and to be a Christian means that we never journey alone. Nothing could be truer. Christianity is a communal faith; we see ourselves as "a people." This concept is deeply rooted in the Judeo-Christian tradition. In the Hebrew Scriptures the metaphor for the binding of many persons into one people is "covenant." The relationship between God and Israel has always been understood in terms of the covenant, a free agreement that has God as its author. God invites Israel to be his people, the people of God, and Israel responds primarily in the Exodus–Sinai experience under the leadership of Moses (see Exod. 19–24 and 33).

God did not make a covenant with individual Hebrews one by one, but with a people. Individuals were part of this covenant because they belonged to the "covenanted community."

God made a pledge to the covenant in terms of God's loving kindness, mercy, and fidelity, but God also demanded these same three qualities from Israel and the Israelites, in terms of their relationship with God and with each other. When Israel was unfaithful to the covenant, God called her back through prophets, exile, and catastrophes. Israel's fidelity to the covenant was not only spiritual: keeping the Torah/Law. God's covenant was also existential: loving kindness, caring for the *Anawin,* the poor of God (orphans, widows, and aliens), and dealing justly with fellow Israelites.

To be human is to be on a journey, and to be a Christian means that we never journey alone.

When Jesus was asked about the greatest commandment, "he cited Deuteronomy 6, as any faithful Jew would have done: love God with all you have and are. Also in keeping with his tradition, he indicated that how we treat one another is integral to our relationship with God."[7] Obviously, our fidelity to the covenant affects the way we relate to God, to ourselves, to others, and to the world. The balance and health of all our relationships were part of God's plan from the beginning. As I explained in chapter 1, it is in and through these four relationships that we live out our spirituality.

As Christians, we never journey alone; we belong to one another. The Gospel according to John records this prayer of Jesus in his final hour: "I pray not only for them, but also for those who will believe in me through their word, so that they may all be one, as you, Father, are in me and I in you, that they also may be in us, that the world may believe that you sent me" (17:20–21). Our unity is not an option; we are bound together in one Body.

Three months ago I was rushed to the hospital with a high fever. In the emergency room they diagnosed a urinary tract infection and loaded me with antibiotics. My doctor was contacted, and he ordered several tests. I ended up in the hospital for eight days and underwent an emergency gall bladder surgery.

There were a few minor complications, but everything went well with one exception: I had a panic attack for the first time in a hospital. I honestly like hospitals, and I have done a lot of pastoral care in hospitals. Yet something happened in the middle of the night that first night, and I was determined to escape the place even if I had my I.V. tubes hanging from my arms. Common sense and the presence of God convinced me that it was stupid to run away, take a taxi to my home in the middle of the night, just to turn around and come back because I was sick and running a high fever. In a moment of clarity, I decided that I had to stay in the hospital. The fascinating part happened next. It did not occur to me to call any member of my family, but I spent the night calling different members of my community until one of them appeared in my room at 5:30 a.m. One of the sisters in the Pastoral Care department also showed up a bit later.

In this moment of unreasonable terror, I needed people who would remind me of the Light and help me turn it on so that the darkness that had overcome me and my hospital room could be dispelled. They listened to my childish fears with respect, they prayed, they blessed me, they brought me a Diet Coke; and by their very presence, I knew that all was well. The "church" was with me.

We have laughed a lot about the episode, and I have told the story to other members of the community. The miracle was that not one of them questioned for a minute the sanity of my telephone calls throughout the night. It was taken for granted that I was in need of the real presence of Jesus, and they were the ones to provide it. We were church.

We often forget that the English word "church" translates the Greek word *ekklēsia,* which designates a gathering of people. In the early years of Christianity, a church building was not called a church, but "the house of the church," thus making clear that the church was truly a gathered people.[8]

A great metaphor for community is given to us by St. Paul in his First Letter to the Corinthians (12:12–27). Paul uses the image of the human body to explain Christ's relationship with believers, and he applies this model to the church, which is the community of the believers. By baptism all, despite diversity of ethnic or social origins, are integrated into one living organism. Paul explains the need for diversity of function among the parts of a body without threat to its unity.

Contextual

One of the dangers we face when trying to communicate with one another is to present ideas or phrases out of their context. Some people use quotes from the Bible to prove what they want to prove even if the quote is completely taken out of context. "Born again," "cut off your hand," "pluck out your eye," etc., are dramatic examples of verses found in Scriptures that cannot be taken literally but need to be read in their context. Every written word or text is surrounded by other parts that can throw light on its meaning.

In the same way, experiences of God and spirituality are colored by our context, that is, our personalities, education, place of birth, childhood events, gifts, limitations, etc. Christian spirituality is by its very nature contextual because it is rooted in the Incarnation. In the person of Jesus the Christ, God's self-communication took on historical and social overtones. Those who knew the historical Jesus were deeply immersed in a sociocultural context.

Jesus experienced the "limitations" of his cultural milieu. The Gospel according to John narrates the moment in which Philip said to Nathanael, "We have found the one about whom Moses wrote in the law, and also the prophets, Jesus, son of Joseph, from Nazareth." But Nathanael said to him, "Can anything good come from Nazareth?" (John 1:45–46). Obviously, the town in which Jesus had been raised did not seem important enough to produce a Messiah. In taking human flesh, Jesus experienced discrimination because of his insignificant origins. The Incarnate Word took on a particular cultural, historical, and social context with all its gifts and limitations.

In order to make his message understood, Jesus borrowed from his surroundings and the familiar experiences of his peers to teach in parables. These stories are a perfect example of Jesus' use of the symbols of his time to communicate God's love in a contextually relevant manner. Our interpretation of the experience of God needs to take into consideration the context in which it happens and the specific perspectives of those who are interpreting it.

I know many ordinary people who take the spiritual journey seriously, but who have not found either the space or the guidance necessary to identify, name, own, and nurture their experiences of God. Jesuit Philip Sheldrake writes:

> We need to come to a realization that all human attempts to respond to the initiative of God... are to some extent limited by particular historical, social and cultural contexts and spiritualities embody specific social values and commitments.[9]

I think the best way to illustrate spirituality as contextual is a personal anecdote. I remember as an adolescent in my native Cuba getting excited about some of the stories I read about Ignacio de Loyola and Teresa de Avila. Their world of knights, honor, kings, and queens spoke to my imagination as a child of Spanish descent. My grandmother used to tell me stories about her great-grandfather, who had fought as a captain in the Spanish Armada during the reign of Ferdinand and Isabella. His many acts of courage had won him the Cruz de San Hermenegildo, apparently a great honor in those days, a medal shaped in the form of a cross (*cruz*). I used to wear this cross on a necklace all the time, for me a symbol not of Christian values or commitment, but of my ancestor's bravery and honor. I was very proud of it.

I know many ordinary people who take the spiritual journey seriously, but who have not found either the space or the guidance necessary to identify, name, own, and nurture their experiences of God.

When I migrated from Cuba at age sixteen, I had to leave all my possessions behind, including my beloved cross. I still remember the sadness and the sense of loss I felt when I took it off from around my neck. Somehow, at that very moment, my world of knights and Spanish chivalry gave way to a different context. I was now a political refugee, an exile, an alien, a stranger. My spirituality changed dramatically, after all, the Cruz de San Hermenegildo was lost forever. As my circumstances changed, I changed, and so did my image of God.

I began to relate to the experience of exile of the Israelites, to their pain and sense of isolation as they sat by the rivers of Babylon weeping, I, like the Israelites, was unable to sing songs of my Spanish/Cuban God in a foreign land (see Ps. 137:1–4). Yet just as Yahweh was there for the chosen people, so was Yahweh also there for me. *The triumphant Lord* of my youth could not hold my faith anymore. A new image began to emerge from those early days of confused identity and boundaries. I came to know the Word of God through whom all things were made, as One who did not regard equality with God as something to be exploited, but emptied himself and became vulnerable with us. I discovered the God who cried when Lazarus died and when he saw Mary and the other Jews weeping; a God who, in Jesus, faced rejection, humiliation, and misunderstanding (John 1:1–11; Phil. 2:6–7; John 11:33; 14:9). This God of my exile had little in common with "His Majesty," as Teresa de Avila used to call him, or as I had also come to image God during my younger years in Cuba. My image and my experience of God changed as the context of my life changed. Not better, not worse, simply different.

For centuries the Eurocentric understanding of spirituality has dominated the United States Catholic Church. We know that some of its elements were shaped by their specific contexts, and yet they are often presented as normative with total disregard for different cultural contexts and experiences. To ignore the contextual dynamic of the faith of today's Christians is to deny an important Incarnational dimension of our faith. The tendency to focus on a single cultural experience of God prevents today's Christians from identifying and naming their own spiritualities. Without them the health of the Christian community is in jeopardy.

Every generation has its spiritual giants. Ours is no different, and in order for these men and women to emerge today we need to stop setting norms that do not speak to their lived experiences. Today's Christians need to look to the past and learn from the best that it has to offer. The challenge is to do it without becoming clones of the classical mystics.

> Part of the contemporary problem with defining "spirituality" is associated with the fact that it is not a single, transcultural, phenomenon but rather is rooted within the lived experience of God's presence in history — and a history that is always specific. Indeed, our basic understanding

of what is "spiritual" and what is "the Christian life" depends, in part at least, on particular experiences rather than merely on a theological language given for all time.[10]

In the thirteenth century we find one of those spiritual giants: Francis of Assisi. Francis questioned whether he should become a hermit or a monk. God broke through the traditional boundaries and used Clare and some of the brothers to say to Francis: "I want you out there, with the people, telling all creation of my unconditional love revealed in Jesus the Christ." Francis became a medieval fool for Christ, a herald of God, a pauper in the streets, a servant preacher. He visited the pope as well as the Sultan, and all creation was his brother and sister. Francis embraced the love for the crucified Christ and his Gospel with the same enthusiasm he had before embraced fun and the passionate desire to fight in the local feudal wars. His impulsive, extroverted, and attractive personality made many young men join him in the early days of his evangelical lifestyle. Although Francis turned the entire world into his monastery and changed the monastic paradigm, he was still influenced by his culture, personality, and medieval customs.

Another example is Teresa de Cepeda y Ahumada, born in 1515 in Avila, Spain. Her paternal grandfather, Juan de Toledo, was a Jewish convert to Christianity and was condemned by the Spanish Inquisition for allegedly returning to the Jewish faith. Her father bought a knighthood and successfully assimilated into Christian society. Teresa's mother, Beatriz, was determined to raise her daughter as a good Catholic. Teresa was fascinated by the lives of the saints and by a world of knights and holy wars. At the age of seven she and her brother ran away from home to find martyrdom among the Moors.

Every generation has its spiritual giants. Ours is no different, and in order for these men and women to emerge today we need to stop setting norms that do not speak to their lived experiences.

Teresa of Avila is perhaps the writer per excellence on contemplative prayer. Her definition is used in the *Catechism of the Catholic Church:* "Contemplative prayer [*oración mental*] in my opinion is nothing else than a close sharing between friends; it means taking time frequently to be alone with him who we know loves us." Contemplative prayer seeks him "whom

my soul loves."[11] Teresa restructured the boundaries
of prayer for her generation by calling Christians
to find God within them rather than outside. Her
passionate, feminine, exuberant, and often criticized
approach to the spiritual life could be a precious
contribution to our often comatose parishes.

The legacy of these spiritual giants needs to be a
prominent part of our spirituality books. Yet they
would be the first to avoid any semblance of spiritual elitism. It is known that Teresa wanted ordinary,
healthy, generous girls for her convents. She was
convinced that all the young women "who were
accepted and who learned to live the life of the
discalced Carmelite were candidates for advanced
prayer, including the kind of spiritual betrothal and
mystical marriage she herself experienced."[12] This
was the opinion of Teresa de Avila; yet today some
still argue that contemplation is not for everyone.

The teachings and experiences of these mystics
were influenced by their particular contexts. Today
we need to continue the search for what constitutes
the essential in our spirituality and let go of the
accidentals that have been fashioned by particular
contexts different from ours. In this specific historical moment we must listen more to one another and
allow the wisdom already present in us to surface. We

are invited to open up to new voices that are waiting to revitalize the Christian community, all those
voices that have not made it to the spirituality books:
lay people's voices, Third World voices, the voices of
the simple, the poor, and the minorities. This third
millennium demands that "anyone who has an ear
listen to what the Spirit is saying to the churches"
(Rev. 3:22).

_____

Chapter Three

The Christian Community

They devoted themselves to the apostles' teach-
ing and fellowship, to the breaking of bread and
the prayers. — Acts 2:42

H OW DO WE DESCRIBE the community that Jesus
dreamed about when he slept under the stars
over two thousand years ago? The Acts of the Apostles
gives us a very succinct definition of these early groups
of believers and their lifestyles.

Acts and the Gospel according to St. Luke were
written by the same author around the years 80–
90. In Acts, Luke offers a brief history of the early
church's development from the resurrection of Jesus
to Paul's first Roman imprisonment. Using Acts, the
early Letters, and my pastoral experience, I offer
some ideas about the meaning of community, what
it is not and what it is.

A Group. A number of assembled individuals,
whether they are riding a bus or a train, sitting in
a theater, or attending a baseball game, are a group.

They do not talk to each other and may not even know the person sitting next to them. If they happen to meet, it is purely by accident.

A Team. A team is a group of people who associate to work together for a common goal. This model is seen in sports, corporations, and certain professions that require a team approach, for example, firefighters, police officers, and medical staff in a hospital. In order to achieve success each member gives more attention to team efforts than to individual achievement.

A Community. According to *Webster's Collegiate Dictionary,* a community is "a unified body of individuals; people with common interests living in a particular area; a body of persons or nations having a common history or common social, economic, and political interests; etc." It is obvious that a community shares more things "in common" than a group or a team. And yet a Christian community is much more than this.

A Christian Community. A Christian community is the web of relationships that provides the sacred, safe space where all members can discover and develop their uniqueness, their giftedness, and their belovedness. It is the locus where God, acting through others, removes the scales from our eyes so that we can discover God's presence in every aspect and dimension of our lives. Through this process, we become *seers* of God in everything and in everyone and this vision impels us to go out of ourselves to serve others.

Unfortunately, this is not often the reality in our parishes. For many people, groups and communities are the same thing. When Christians gather for one reason or another, they call themselves a group or a community depending on their purpose for meeting and their commitment to each other's spiritual growth. We hear, for example, members of a Cursillo or a Charismatic Prayer group call themselves a community. On the other hand, the process of Renew International, which aims to form faith communities, tends to call these gatherings "group meetings."

To understand Christian community, we must go back to the beginnings of the young Christian church and reflect on the different elements that constituted then and now a Christian community.

※

Christians did not invent the concept of community. When the Roman conquest put an end to Greek democracy, most citizens lost their public voice. This situation gave birth to a new social structure to mediate between the family and the larger society. It was called *koinonia*, a Greek word that means partnership or fellowship. The first usage of *koinonia* in the Greek New Testament is found in Acts 2:42–46, where we read a striking description of the common life shared by the early Christian believers in Jerusalem:

> They devoted themselves to the teaching of the apostles and to the communal life [*koinonia*], to the breaking of the bread and to the prayers. Awe came upon everyone, and many wonders and signs were done through the apostles. All who believed were together and had all things in common; they would sell their property and possessions and divide them among all according to each one's need. Every day they devoted themselves to meeting together in the temple area and to breaking bread in their homes. They ate their meals with exultation and sincerity of heart.

Koinonia was already a social reality in the Greek world where Christian communities began forming. Although it was not a religious structure, it provided a model for the early Christian faith communities. We can say that *koinonia* speaks of community, inner relationships, and the active participation in social affairs. Interestingly, the meaning of the word always implies action and also assumes the presence of a spirit of generous giving as contrasted with selfish getting.

There are many models and ways of speaking about community. As a Cuban-American, I can easily associate the concept with that of family because, for me, both should aim at a common healthy unity. Healthy families and communities strive for healing, unity, and respect among its members. At the beginning of this chapter, I defined community as "the place that provides the sacred, safe space where all members can discover and develop their uniqueness, their giftedness, and their belovedness." But community is not just "a place"; it is a living organism, dynamic, alive, and always changing, just like a family.

In the ideal family, members enable each other to discover and develop their uniqueness and their talents, but above all, each one is loved, accepted, and valued by the rest. In a healthy family system, the role of each member is not defined by his or her level of productivity, but by the love that is given and received. My grandmother may be confused and forget my name; she may even "smell and drool," but she will always be my grandmother, and I would never consider "getting rid of her" because she has turned annoying in her old age.

This is the unity that Catholics celebrate in the Eucharist, the sacrament of communion with one another in the one body of Christ. St. Thomas Aquinas wrote in his *Summa Theologica*: "the Eucharist is the sacrament of the unity of the Church, which results from the fact that many are one in Christ."[13] This is the oneness, the unity that Jesus prayed for before entering his passion and death. But unity does not mean uniformity or agreement on every issue, as we will see in chapter 4. This unity is the one that Paul spoke about: ears, hands, eyes, feet, and arms — all working together and sharing a diversity of gifts for the good of the Body.

In a healthy family system, the role of each member is not defined by his or her level of productivity, but by the love that is given and received.

The best time to experience this unity is during hurricane season in South Florida. Anyone who has experienced hurricanes, storms, tornadoes, or any other natural disaster will immediately know what I mean. Neighbors of all races, backgrounds, political ideologies, or languages came together to help one another. During one of the last hurricanes that hit Florida, we were without power for over two weeks. We were hot and living on cold canned foods. One of the neighbors, of Czechoslovakian ancestry, married to a woman from Colombia, came to tell us that he had a generator. He offered to connect two of our power outlets to it: the refrigerator and the light in one of the rooms. Alleluia! These people we hardly knew used their gasoline so that our food would not spoil and we could have some light in the house. We shared meals with strangers, and spent most of the evenings outside without the protection of our air conditioners. Those of us who had enough gas in our cars went to the places where the Red Cross was distributing water and brought it back for everyone in the block. It was one of the great blessings of the storm. We lost our roof, trees, the fence, the electrical box, etc., but we also gained many friends that we had not discovered before. Our diversity of gifts was the greatest asset and we were able to live the unity without uniformity of which Paul spoke so eloquently.

>|<

The second element required for a community to be Christian has to do with the Good News of Jesus Christ. John the Baptist announced the coming of the Reign of God. Jesus inaugurated it and made it a reality. The Good News proclaims this Reign of love, peace, justice, forgiveness, and compassion. This is the message of the inclusivity of God's love, the God who, in Jesus, embraced sinners, lepers, women, and the marginalized of society. This is the Good News of God's desire for us, for our healing, for the restoration of the relationship with God and with each other. This Good News is the foundation of the Christian community and it requires more than just believing it. The early communities were never passive; they were not just about "being" together, but also about "doing" together.

The message of Jesus is to be proclaimed; the story needs to be retold over and over. This dimension is known as *kerygma*, the Greek word used in the New Testament for preaching, also related to the Greek verb meaning to cry or proclaim as a herald.

A Christian community not only relies on the quality of the relationships among its members; it also has to be grounded in the proclamation of the Good News of Jesus Christ. In chapter 2, I emphasized the importance of contextualizing religious experiences to remain open to new voices. Yet there are some elements that are foundational to the Christian faith and are also transcultural.

Christians believe in one God, Creator of all. We believe in Jesus, the Incarnate Word of God, the beginning and the end, the "image of the invisible God, the firstborn of all creation" (Col. 1:15). The Incarnation is central to the Christian faith.

We do believe in the Holy Spirit whose temples we are and who comforts, guides, and strengthens us. We believe in the church as the Body of Christ, the communion of the saints, the forgiveness of sins, and eternal life.

Moreover, we believe that the God that Jesus came to reveal "is Love" (1 John 4:16); compassionate, forgiving, inclusive, and willing to suffer with and for us. We believe that this faith is not just a relationship with God "above" but with ourselves, with others, and with all of creation. This is our faith, the faith of the church, and it does transcend all contexts and cultures.

Many Christians gather regularly to pray together. Prayer is the starting point of any action and also our way to remain connected to God, but this richness is not to be kept under a table. I have noticed that some Catholics are hesitant to name their beliefs. They still see religion as a personal thing that should not be imposed on anyone. Pope Paul VI, in his encyclical *Evangelii Nuntiandi,* called each Christian not to impose, but to propose the Good News of the love of God.

I watch the news every day or read it on the Internet; I want to be in touch with what is happening in my global home earth. I hear about all the bad things that are slowly killing the earth and my brothers and sisters around the world, but I seldom hear hopeful alternatives or suggestions to make it all better, to bring some healing to our wounded world. The Gospel message, the power of "God is with us," the Good News that we are not alone and that there is a purpose to life other than money, is not being proclaimed. True, a few speak of it in the megachurches on T.V. where if you contribute enough money the gospel promises riches, health, and a long life — but this is not the Christian message.

Not too many people proclaim that Jesus is sharing the pain of the unemployed, of those who have lost their life savings, or are terminally ill. This Christian hope has been successfully placed under a bushel basket by those of us who should be proclaiming it.

✦|✦

There is a third element easily identified in the early communities: the celebration in ritual of their common faith. We know it as liturgy (*leitourgia*), a Greek composite word "meaning originally a public duty, a service to the state undertaken by a citizen."[14] The quotation from the Book of Acts on page 67 reminds us that the early Christians devoted themselves "to the breaking of the bread and to the prayers." The breaking of the bread was the initial way of designating what we know today as the Holy Mass or the Eucharistic Celebration.

Unfortunately today, some Catholics neglect this aspect of our faith. The "breaking of the bread" was the central reason for the gathering of the early Christians and ultimately a major factor for being excommunicated from Judaism. Initially, Christianity was another sect of Judaism: the "Nazareans," or the followers of "the Way." They attended the local synagogues on the Sabbath to listen to the Scriptures (Old Testament), and then gathered in their homes on Sunday (the Day of the Lord) for the breaking of the bread and the fellowship. Eventually, the Jewish religious authorities realized that these people could not be considered Jews anymore, because when they gathered on Sundays, they sang hymns praising Christ as Lord (God).

Whatever changes Catholic spirituality has experienced through the ages, the celebration of the Eucharist remains the center and the summit of our worship. The Eucharist is seldom celebrated in small Christian communities; still, the element of *leitourgia* is expressed through common prayer.

A priest friend told me one morning over a cup of coffee after the Eucharist: "I wish people understood how hard it is to celebrate and preach with a group of unconverted Catholics." His comments made me wonder, I had never thought about this from a priest's perspective. Most Catholics have been sacramentalized, but that does not mean they know God or understand the demands of being a disciple of Jesus. Of course, we all know that some clergy do not know it either.

Whatever changes Catholic spirituality has experienced through the ages, the celebration of the Eucharist remains the center and the summit of our worship.

People go to Mass for many different reasons, but the complaints that I have heard during many years in ministry are similar: "I can't stand that choir! They are only making noise, and it bothers my prayer; I am going to have to go to another parish." "That priest doesn't even know how to talk; he mumbles to himself; do I come to church for this?" "The number of Hispanics, blacks, Asians, poor, [whatever] is growing; I am going to start looking for another church."

These words remind me of people who go to a wedding but do not know the bride or the groom. Some members of my community and I went to the wedding of one of the members. The bride and the groom were young, poor, and unsophisticated. By human standards, the event was a disaster. The bride was late and the parish had a Confirmation rehearsal planned immediately following the ceremony. Because of tight scheduling, we could not have a Mass as planned and the priest distributed Communion hurriedly. We all got lost getting to the reception hall and arrived tired, thirsty, and hungry. After an hour of waiting, without any food or drink, the bride and the groom made their glorious entrance. We clapped and shouted and expressed our joy to the best of our abilities given the tight space. When we finally sat, a boom box began to play music, and the happy couple started to dance, with a few other couples eventually joining them.

Close to midnight, someone announced that "dinner would be served in a few seconds"; we rejoiced! After a moment some ladies dressed like table servers appeared carrying trays filled with boxes of fried chicken that were promptly distributed among all the guests. I admit I did not know whether to laugh, cry, or faint. Suddenly, someone sitting with me said, "Isn't this a great idea? Serving like this is fast, everyone has his or her own box, and it already has napkins, dinnerware, and the little wet thing to clean our fingers." The comment was echoed by everyone at my table, and it soon spread all over the hall. The consensus was that given the youth and the limitations of the couple, they had done an outstanding job, and the entire night had been a success.

The only reason that a group of intelligent people were able to declare this night a success was because we knew and loved the bride and the groom. We were willing to ignore all the mistakes to focus on the real reason that brought us together: the celebration of the birth of a young Christian family. It is my belief that many of us sitting in church on Sunday do not have a relationship with Christ, the host, and therefore are unable to rejoice and celebrate unless all the external paraphernalia are perfect and enjoyable.

⁂

The fourth and last element that makes up a Christian community is *diakonia*, from the Greek word meaning service. Traditionally, Catholics associate this word with the role of deacons and their position in the church's organizational structure. Indeed, according to the tradition of the Catholic Church, the narrative of Acts 6:1–6 describes the institution of the office of deacon. *Diakonia* (or service), however, is an integral part of the Gospel message. When Jesus talked about it, he was not referring to a specific ministry within the church, but to the calling of all his disciples, the mark of his followers:

You know that those who are recognized as rulers over the Gentiles lord it over them, and their great ones make their authority over them felt. But it shall not be so among you. Rather, whoever wishes to be great among you will be your servant; whoever wishes to be first among you will be the slave of all. For the Son of Man did not come to be served but to serve. (Mark 10:42–45)

No community deserves to be known as Christian if their praying, sharing, celebrating, and proclaiming are not wrapped in a blanket of active service to each other and to the world.

In the Letter to the Galatians, Paul reminds his readers that they were called for freedom, and that this freedom should not be abused to do whatever they pleased; but rather, to "serve one another through love. For the whole law is fulfilled in one statement, namely, 'You shall love your neighbor as yourself'" (Gal. 5:13–14).

The entire Gospel message is a call to love, conversion, forgiveness, compassion, and service. No community deserves to be known as Christian if their praying, sharing, celebrating, and proclaiming are not wrapped in a blanket of active service to each other and to the world. Today's small Christian communities usually call this dimension "mission," because it takes everyone outside their personal worlds and into the needs of others, not only in their community, but also in their family, workplace, parish, neighborhood, and wider society. The Gospel according to Matthew provides us with a very powerful message:

> When the Son of Man comes in his glory. . . . All the nations will be gathered before him, and he will separate people one from another as a shepherd separates the sheep from the goats, and he will put the sheep at his right hand and the goats at the left. Then the king will say to those at his right hand, "Come, you that are blessed by my Father, inherit the kingdom prepared for you from the foundation of the world; for I was hungry and you gave me food, I was thirsty and you gave me something to drink, I was a stranger and you welcomed me, I was naked and you gave me clothing, I was sick and you took care of me, I was in prison and you visited me." Then the righteous will answer him, "Lord, when was it that we saw you hungry and gave you food, or

thirsty and gave you something to drink? And when was it that we saw you a stranger and welcomed you, or naked and gave you clothing? And when was it that we saw you sick or in prison and visited you?" And the king will answer them, "Truly I tell you, just as you did it to one of the least of these who are members of my family, you did it to me." Then he will say to those at his left hand, "You that are accursed depart from me into the eternal fire prepared for the devil and his angels; for I was hungry and you gave me no food, I was thirsty and you gave me nothing to drink...." Then they also will answer, "Lord, when was it that we saw you hungry or thirsty or a stranger or naked or sick or in prison, and did not take care of you?" Then he will answer them, "Truly I tell you, just as you did not do it to one of the least of these, you did not do it to me." And these will go away into eternal punishment, but the righteous into eternal life. (Matt. 25:31–46)

These are harsh and disturbing words and yet they clearly outline some of the implications of the Incarnation. If we are to see God in all and all in God, if we believe that we are the temples of the Spirit of

God, then service to others, washing their feet, is not an option. The First Letter of John is clear:

> God is love, and those who abide in love abide in God, and God abides in them.... We love because he first loved us. Those who say, "I love God," and hate their brothers or sisters, are liars; for those who do not love a brother or sister whom they have seen, cannot love God whom they have not seen. The commandment we have from him is this: those who love God must love their brothers and sisters also. (4:16, 19–21)

If we are to see God in all and all in God, if we believe that we are the temples of the Spirit of God, then service to others, washing their feet, is not an option.

A true Christian community must be involved in the needs of its parish, neighborhood, country, and world. There are no geographical or racial boundaries for those who claim to believe in Immanuel, God with us. God is with us, within us, and among us, and anything we do or fail to do to one another we do it to God.

To Summarize

- When Jesus taught his disciples to pray he said, "Our Father...." The implication of the parent-hood of God is that it relates us to one another. Earlier, when I used the image of a family applied to the church, I was keenly aware that, in a family, we have no say in who would be a member; we cannot pick and choose only those people that we like. I believe that Jesus had a similar idea when he basically called us "siblings" whether we liked it or not.

The early community had serious difficulties with this concept, and that prompted Paul to write chapters 11, 12, and 13 of his First Letter to the Corinthians. Out of the tensions, quarrels, and selfishness of the Corinthians the concept of the Body of Christ was born. Drawing a masterful analogy between the human body and the Body of Christ, the church, Paul explains in detail the absurdity of denying the value of each member and the diverse role each plays. In the Letter to the Romans he affirms, "For as in one body we have many parts, and all the parts do not have the same function, so we, though many, are one body in Christ and individually parts of one another" (Rom. 12:4–5). Unity is so rare in today's society. Everyone longs for it, but not too many are willing to pay the price to make it a reality. In chapters 4 and 5, I will offer a few thoughts on the topic of unity in diversity.

• The Christian community is charged with the mandate to retell the Story. Fellowship and sound relationships without the proclamation of the Good News would shortchange the mystery of community, which is at the heart of the message. If we are willing to be compassionate with each other, to consider even the "ailing and frail" members as parts of the Body, it is only because we are sure of God's love for us all. Giving each other the gift of our belovedness is the greatest task of a community, and that can be accomplished only because we believe that God loved us first (1 John 4:19). This Good News ought to be proclaimed at all times.

• It is hard to live the values of the Gospel in our society. That is why we need to come together to support each other's faith. One of the best ways to do that is to gather as the Community of the Believers to celebrate our faith in prayer and ritual. Whether in the Eucharistic meal or in any other liturgical celebration, Christians need to come together and express, share, affirm, and ritualize their beliefs.

In community Christians find strength. Jesus' desire and determination to find the lost sheep was motivated by his wish to bring the flock together. The call to community is the gift and the challenge of Christianity.

The Spirituality of Community

*As a body is one though it has many parts, and
all the parts of the body, though many, are one
body, so also Christ. For in one Spirit we were all
baptized into one body, whether Jews or Greeks,
slaves or free persons, and we were all given to
drink of one Spirit.*

— 1 Corinthians 12:12–13

M OST CATHOLICS ARE FAMILIAR with this pas-
sage of Scripture. What many do not know
is how connected this chapter is to the preceding
and to the following chapters of the Letter. In chapter 11, Paul criticizes the people of Corinth for the
way they conduct themselves in their religious assem-
blies, when they come together for the "breaking of
the bread." In the first century these were the early
household churches and they continued to meet in
homes until the fourth century.

In chapter 11:17–34, Paul touches on one of the
most serious abuses connected with the celebration

of the Eucharist. It had been reported to him that at the *agape* celebration preceding the celebration of the Eucharist, the mutual sharing of food and fellowship was being violated by neglecting the needy. More-over, some members were getting drunk during the celebration. Obviously, the community was ignoring the basic Christian tradition concerning the mean-ing of the Lord's Supper. Paul recalled that tradition for them and reminded them of its implications. His words are strong,

> When you meet in one place, then, it is not to eat the Lord's Supper, for in eating, each one goes ahead with his own supper, and one goes hungry while another gets drunk. Do you not have houses in which you can eat and drink? Or do you show contempt for the church of God and make those who have nothing feel ashamed? What can I say to you? Shall I praise you? In this matter I do not praise you. (11:20–22)

The following verses (23–26) contain the earliest account of the institution of the Lord's Supper in the New Testament, written before the Gospels.

Paul issues a stern warning to those who "eat and drink without recognizing the body," because they "eat and drink a judgment on themselves" (11:29). If we were to hear this kind of comment in one of our parishes today, we would assume that the person was not showing respect for the Sacred Host and for the Blood of Christ. Paul implies that Corinthians were not showing the proper respect for the celebration of the Lord's Supper, but it does not mean that they were denying the Real Presence of Christ in the bread and the wine. Rather, they were abusing and "showing contempt for the church of God," the Body of Christ. This is where chapter 12 continues:

> Now the body is not a single part, but many. If a foot should say, "Because I am not a hand I do not belong to the body," it does not for this reason belong any less to the body. Or if an ear should say, "Because I am not an eye I do not belong to the body," it does not for this reason belong any less to the body. If the whole body were an eye, where would the hearing be? If the whole body were hearing, where would the sense of smell be? But as it is, God placed the parts, each one of them, in the body as he intended. If they were all one part, where would the body be? But as it is, there are many parts, yet one body.

Chapter 12 emerges out of Paul's attempt to explain the right relationships between the members of the churches. The analogy between the human body and the Body of Christ (the church) is a literary and theological masterpiece. After emphasizing the importance of respecting all members, of the interconnectedness of all, and of the unity in diversity, Paul writes his famous chapter 13 about love. This is the logical and perfect ending for this portion of the Letter. Christians are not showing respect for each other, relationships are being destroyed, and competition about the gifts and charisms is damaging the community. Paul reminds them of the reason they come together and encourages them to change their behavior. He finishes emphasizing that no matter what heroic acts they were performing or how awesome their gifts were, without love they were nothing. This is a strong reminder of the communal nature of God, the Divine Lover, and of the community of the beloved disciples.

I had the opportunity to see this reading dramatized analogically in my own experience.

A few years ago I went to the White Mountains of New Hampshire with my family. Anyone who has been there knows the beautiful trails that fill a hiker's heart with joy. The children were young and full of energy and so we took on the challenge. What I had not shared with anyone was that for several weeks I had been suffering from an ingrown toenail in my big toe. I had tried the usual home remedies but nothing seemed to improve the condition.

What do we do with the members of the Body of Christ who cause us pain? Do we give them some space so that they do not hurt so much? Or do we ignore, reject, and get rid of them?

After a couple of hours in my hiking boots my toe was throbbing. I could hardly walk and was slowing down the group. The ordeal continued as my pain was becoming unbearable, and the children were getting more frustrated with my pace. Finally, my brother stopped and said, "Sit on that rock and give me your boot." In shock, I watched him cut off the entire top front part of my leather boot with his hunting knife. After a few minutes of handiwork, he gave it back to me and said, "Here, the toe won't bother you anymore; it has all the space it needs to move freely without hurting." The rest of the trip was uneventful.

The experience has stayed with me all these years. How many "ingrown toenails" are in the Body of Christ? How many members of the Body seem to bring only pain, infection, and frustration to the rest of us? The image of my brother working on my shoe to accommodate my toe taught me a lesson.

What do we do with the members of the Body of Christ who cause us pain? Do we try to heal them and make them comfortable? Do we give them some space so that they do not hurt so much? Or do we ignore, reject, and get rid of them? Do we punish them with our indifference or neglect?

The Letter to the Romans tells us, "None of us lives for oneself, and no one dies for oneself" (14:7). And 1 Corinthians adds, "If one part suffers, all the parts suffer with it; if one part is honored, all the parts share its joy. Now you are Christ's body, and individually parts of it" (12:26–27).

My ingrown toenail showed me how poorly I deal with the members of my other Body. I get impatient and do not even offer them an ointment or a Band-Aid for their pain. The Christian God revealed by Jesus is full of compassion and demands that same compassion from us.

The measure of the quality of a Christian community is the way in which its weakest members are treated and the willingness to welcome everyone as an important part of the Body of Christ.

I am involved in developing small Christian communities within parishes. In addition, I work with interparochial intentional communities composed of people who share a similar spirituality. Some of these communities are homogeneous and frequently share a common language. Others are as diverse as can be imagined. One of them is made up of people from Puerto Rico, Haiti, Italy, Dominican Republic, and Cuba, as well as Euro-Americans of German, Italian, Scottish, and Irish backgrounds. Yet in spite of our differences I can say that we are of "one heart and mind." Do we always agree on every issue or respond the same way to a stimulus? Of course not. But we are keenly aware that we need one another and that when one member is missing the Body is incomplete.

In chapter 3, I defined community as "the web of relationships that provides the sacred, safe space where all members can discover and develop their uniqueness, their giftedness, and their belovedness. It is the locus where God, acting through others, removes the scales from our eyes so that we can discover God's presence in every aspect and dimension of our lives. Through this process, we become *seers* of God in everything and in everyone and this vision impels us to go out of ourselves to serve others."

I cannot remember how often my community has helped me to be more honest and true to whom I am. There are times when I wander away from my true self, and they remind me of my call to faithfulness.

Many other times, when I am suffering from "acute perfectionitis," they call me back to faithfulness and away from the frustration and the danger of desiring human perfection. At the end of the day, none of our communities is "perfect" from the human standpoint, but they all strive to be faithful.

Christian Communities Are Always on a Journey of Hope

There are other elements that play a central role in the spirituality of Christian communities. I emphasize the concepts of journey and hope because I believe that they are foundational to the spirituality of community. Community is not a static concept, but a dynamic reality, always in a process of conversion and transformation. Each journey has ups and downs, moments of grace and moments of sin; the only constant is change, which many of us resist or fear. Yet without change, there can be no conversion, which is at the center of the Christian life.

Hope is what makes the Christian journey possible. We hope because we trust; and we trust because we believe. The source of our hope is God, and God is always with us here and now. In the Bible, this hope is often expressed by the notion of promise, and it seems to point to the future, but hope is also in the present tense. We hope because God *is,* our hope *is* in the God who has made heaven and earth. Thus we embark on our communal journey of hope trusting that it holds the promise and the potential for the transformation of each member and of the community itself.

In my own life in community I have realized that this transformation has two foundations:

1. the belief that each member is the beloved of God, regardless of looks, color, weight, intelligence, economic status, educational level, etc.

2. the conviction that our lives and our everyday experiences have revelatory power.

We Are God's Beloved

In his book *Life of the Beloved,* the late Henri J. M. Nouwen, one of the great spiritual writers of the twentieth century, developed a core concept in spirituality. According to Nouwen, believing that we are the beloved of God is the ultimate truth of our lives, and, in his words, "Isn't that what friendship is all about: giving to each other the gift of our Belovedness?"[15]

The problem is that the voice of God that softly whispers this truth in our hearts has to compete with the loud screams of other voices that shout: "You are ugly, different, dumb, too heavy, too skinny... basically you are unimportant and irrelevant." In my experience, most Christians do not believe in their belovedness and therefore find it very hard to see belovedness in others. Believing in our belovedness is the invitation, the gift, and the challenge of community.

Often our inability to believe in God's unconditional love and constant care makes it impossible to discover God in the ordinary.

I often hear comments such as: "My community is great. We pray the Rosary together, offer our petitions to God, and always close our meetings with an Our Father, a Hail Mary, and a Glory Be. At the end, we have some refreshments." This group may be wonderful and their prayer honest, but are they helping each other to discover and accept their own belovedness? Discovering our value in the eyes of God requires companions on the journey; companions who walk *with us,* not in front or behind; spiritual friends, sojourners who also struggle with their belovedness and giftedness. This kind of relationship is risky and has to rely totally upon God's goodness and upon the power of God's Spirit living in each of us. Christian communities must provide the sacred, safe space where all members can discover and own their belovedness.

Our Lives and Our Everyday Experiences Have Revelatory Power

When was the last time that you "saw" God clearly during a picnic or a birthday party? What was happening in your life the last time you felt God's presence within you? What were you doing?

We want to know God. We want to "see" and "feel" God. We read the Bible, attend church services, spend time before the Blessed Sacrament, and participate in the Eucharist. These are all the ordinary places in which both religion and society tell us that God is. This is true, but there is a whole other aspect that gets neglected.

Our everyday lives and experiences have revelatory power. That is, we can encounter God in births, deaths, joy, unemployment, and illness. We can also find God in ordinary places: home, workplace, civic community, etc. Often our inability to believe in God's unconditional love and constant care makes it impossible to discover God in the ordinary. How could I possibly believe that God is interested in this small person? Accepting that we are God's beloved enables us to see God in everything that is human.

A few months ago I was facilitating a retreat in one of the local parishes. This parish is located in a beautiful area next to a lake and surrounded by large trees. During one of the sessions, I looked outside and saw the pastor playing football with some of the children attending religion classes. I noticed that many of the participants had also been taken by what they saw through the huge picture window in the parish hall.

Filled with curiosity, I asked them: "What do you see?" The first answers came quickly, "Father is playing with the children." I continued, "What else do you see?" Someone responded, "It's a beautiful day. I wish I had brought my camera to capture the moment." I pressed on, "Is that all you see?" A couple of the participants claimed that they were touched by the gentleness of the priest playing with the children.

As I continued my interrogation, I got different kinds of answers: "I am edified by the priest's involvement with the students. I wish every parish had a pastor like ours." Someone offered, "This experience is calling me to be more present to my own children," and so the sharing continued for a few more minutes.

I asked, "Did anyone go beyond what our senses showed us and discover God in the beautiful day, the landscape, the children, or the priest?" Shocked, they confessed, "We were not thinking in religious terms at this moment." Sad...

The mystery of the Incarnation, of which I spoke in chapter 1, assures us that because God became human, humanity is sacred and all that is human reveals God. When a child is born or when a child dies prematurely, when we suffer or rejoice, when we marry and share love, or when we lose a loved one, God *is*. If we believe in the Incarnation, we know that God is in everything and that everything is in God.

It has been said that the psalms are "a school of prayer" that inspire us to voice our own deepest feelings. Such is Psalm 139:7–13.

> Where can I hide from your spirit?
> From your presence, where can I flee?
> If I ascend to the heavens, you are there;
> if I lie down in Sheol, you are there too.
> If I fly with the wings of dawn and alight
>   beyond the sea,
> Even there your hand will guide me,
> your right hand will hold me fast.

> If I say, "Surely darkness shall hide me,
> and night shall be my light" —
> Darkness is not dark for you,
> and night shines as the day.
> Darkness and light are but one.
> You formed my inmost being;
> you knit me in my mother's womb.

This ancient song tells us that God is everywhere, in the darkness and in the light, in the heavens and in Sheol. God is revealed even in the most unusual places and circumstances.

Sadly our society does not support this truth, and often even our churches fail to affirm it. This is why, in an effort to find comfort, security, and the "sacred," we run to places designated as holy, such as churches, synagogues, etc., and look for "holy people" (clergy, religious, and spiritual guides) in search of wisdom. Discovering our belovedness and the revelatory power of our experiences does not happen in isolation. We need others to show us what our eyes cannot see.

There is a story that I read in one of Anthony de Mello's books that goes something like this:

> Once upon a time, there was a very pious woman full of the love of God. She would go to church every morning and usually was approached by

poor children and homeless people, but she was so absorbed in her prayers that she would not be bothered by them.

One day she arrived at the church as the services were just beginning and found the door locked. She was devastated. It would be the first time in years that she would miss her religious services. Filled with sadness, she looked up... and to her surprise, right there in front of her eyes, there was a note taped to the church door. The note read: "I AM OUT THERE!"

The story may be a bit exaggerated, but it is a good illustration of my previous words. Many lay Catholics have difficulty trusting the sacredness of ordinary experiences and even more the active presence of God in the midst of what we may consider common or even unholy. Belonging to a true Christian community can heal us from our spiritual blindness so that we can discover the presence of God in the mess of our lives.

Chapter Five

The Challenge of the Christian Community

Beloved, let us love one another, because love is from God; everyone who loves is born of God and knows God. Whoever does not love does not know God, for God is love....Beloved, since God loved us so much, we also ought to love one another. No one has ever seen God; if we love one another, God lives in us, and his love is perfected in us.

— 1 John 4:7–8, 11–12

THROUGHOUT THIS BOOK, I have consistently maintained that as Catholics we believe in the God of love, compassion, and forgiveness. "God is love," affirms the First Letter of John (4:16), and since we have been created in God's image and likeness, it is fair to assume that we are also love, created by love, in love, and for love. Yet I know from experience that loving is often a challenging proposition within a community and that even if I believe in a loving God, I do not seem to be able to transfer that love to my brothers and sisters. I ask, "Am I a liar as John seems to imply in another section of his Letter?"

I think that I am honest when I struggle to accept everyone in my small community or in my parish. Yet after many years of experience, I have discovered two dynamics operating in each community that can threaten the healthy relationships among its members and consequently block its journey of hope:

1. the growth and transformation of each individual member, and

2. the growth and transformation of the relationships, that is, the actual community life.

The way in which these two dynamics interrelate is frequently the root of tensions and even conflict in the life of a Christian community. By the transformation of the individual, I mean the journey from an anonymous, hopeless person to one who believes in his or her belovedness, who knows he or she has been called and gifted by God, and who has a sense of purpose: a person of hope.

This individual journey can be difficult, rewarding, and at times painful, but it can get very complicated when it meets my brother's or sister's journey. As an individual, my spiritual growth can be slow or fast, hopeful or frustrating, but it is *my* growth. When in addition to my own struggles I have to deal with some else's process, things can get tough. The transformation of the relationships, the actual community life, is born when "my process of transformation" and "someone else's journey" meet.

Often we have difficulty accepting that each person is unique and responds to God's promptings in unique ways. We can remain a community of faith even as we experience complex personal differences such as culture, styles of prayer, political preferences, diverse personalities, etc. Although we belong to the same community, we are not expected to be clones of each other. The invitation is to come together as we are, bringing our own gifts and placing them at the service of the whole. In my inclination to paraphrase Scripture, I can image Jesus saying, "See how they tolerate one another!"

Is this unity in diversity possible? Jesus seemed to believe so when he chose twelve different people and entrusted to them the dream and the mission of the Reign of God. I would have never brought together a tax collector, a fisherman, and a zealot; and yet Jesus did. If he had not, we would not be able to accept today Paul's ideal of the Body of Christ. We cannot be only feet, or ears, or hands, or eyes. As it is, "God placed the parts, each one of them, in the body as he intended. If they were all one part, where would the body be? But as it is, there are many parts, yet one body" (1 Cor. 12:18–20).

A few years ago I had a revealing experience. A young woman shared in her small community that her pastor had invited her to help in the catechetical program. She panicked and told him that she was "unworthy" and unqualified. Everyone listened but no one offered any affirmation or pointed out her many talents. I knew that this lady had a tremendous potential and could not understand her hesitation and the lack of support of her friends. After a while, the issue became clear. Most of the other members of the community belonged to a charismatic prayer group, while she was rather quiet and favored a different style of prayer. With covert "pity" they encouraged her to go through a Life in the Spirit Seminar so that she could "receive" the gifts of the Holy Spirit and become a self-assured catechist.

Situations like this are not unusual. Many Christians believe that there is a way to pray, usually theirs, that is superior to others. We tend to measure or evaluate others' spirituality and prayer style by our own preferences, what works for us, and often ignore the uniqueness of each person. When our "companions" in the journey speak judgmentally or begin to compete about who is right and who is wrong, the transformation of the relationships in the community is endangered.

Christian communities are expected to see value in differences and to discover God in the mystery and uniqueness of each person.

When I was about twenty years old I made my first Spiritual Exercises in the tradition of St. Ignatius of Loyola.[16] The retreat lasted eight days, and I remember spending the first three in total frustration. The priest director gave us readings from Scripture that we were supposed to follow during our several periods of meditation each day. I must say that I really tried. For reasons that eluded me at the time, when I was expected to "meditate" on Jesus' love for Peter even in his weakness, I found myself at the foot of the Cross. If the meditation invited me to "ponder" the scene where Jesus washes the disciples' feet, I would go outside and "consider the lilies. . . . " Moreover, I was finding it almost impossible to "sit and attend to my bodily posture in prayer." After many unsuccessful attempts to follow the Exercises, my guilt began to escalate. Finally, in an act of supreme honesty and humility I told the priest that I was a lousy pray-er and totally unable to "place myself in God's presence" as the retreat required. I remember the expression on his face when he asked me what I was doing with all the free time I had on my hands. Still filled with profound contrition, I confessed: "Since I cannot pray, I go outside and sit by the lake. I look at the water and can almost hear God speaking to me there. I become very attentive because I don't want to miss anything God is saying." The priest smiled encouragingly and asked, "What is God saying to you?" Confused, I responded, "I don't know what God is saying. We are sitting there together, just being. I don't think I hear much or say much. I am so sorry." I always thought he found the whole thing amusing, but I remember the gentleness with which he said: "Don't worry about the readings. God is inviting you to a different form of contemplation, and the important thing is to follow his lead." In my usual inquisitive manner, I asked him: "What is contemplation?" He answered: "Don't worry about that now; just go to the lake and *be* with your God."

After so many years I still smile when I remember this episode. The Jesuit priest directing me was able to let go of the Ignatian method in order to follow the spirit behind the method. I cannot recall every detail of that retreat, but the sense of liberation, of having received "permission" to allow God to be God, has remained at the core of my spirituality.

If true community life depends on the growth and transformation of relationships, then differences and even conflict have to be an integral part of the journey. The temptation in some Christian circles is to deny or ignore conflict as a contradiction to the Gospel lifestyle. To dissipate the tension that conflict creates, we often foster a "pseudo-peace" that makes us feel less guilty about our feelings of frustration or even anger.

Consequently, our communities do not grow because to sustain this pseudo-peace, we encourage an atmosphere of "private" prayer, "individual devotions," and intolerance for diversity. It is difficult to accept that we do not move at the same speed or dance to the same music. Individually, we may all be engaged in the process of transformation, but unless we learn to dance together with different steps Christian community will not happen. In my experience, this is the area where most difficulties arise and growth slows down.

A brief look at our early stories may help heal us from the exaggerated fear of diversity that many of us suffer from today.

> The community of believers was of one heart and mind, and no one claimed that any of his possessions was his own, but they had everything in common.... There was no needy person among them, for those who owned property or

houses would sell them, bring the proceeds of the sale, and put them at the feet of the apostles, and they were distributed to each according to need. (Acts 4:32–35)

This description of community found in the Book of Acts depicts a perfect *koinonia:* people of one heart and mind, sharing everything in common. But as we move to the next chapter we learn the story of Ananias and his wife, Sapphira, who sold a piece of property. They retained some of the purchase price and put the remainder at the feet of the apostles. Peter severely reprimanded them not because they withheld part of the money but because they had deceived the community. Luke narrates that they both died in front of the people (Acts 5:1–11). Jesus' dream of unity lived on in spite of this crisis.

Individually, we may all be engaged in the process of transformation, but unless we learn to dance together with different steps Christian community will not happen.

Soon another conflict developed. Originally considered to be a Jewish sect in Jerusalem, Christian communities began to welcome people of other cultures and religious backgrounds. This was seen as totally irreconcilable with the Jewish faith and caused the final break between Jewish Christians and the synagogue.

Acts 11:26 reports that the disciples of Jesus were first called Christians at Antioch. Antioch's strategic location made it an ideal crossroads for diverse people, languages, religious communities, and cultures. We may conclude that the first Christian communities were as multicultural and diverse as today's communities.

Luke explains that "as the number of disciples continued to grow, the Hellenists [probably Palestinian Jews who spoke only Greek] complained against the Hebrews [Palestinian Jews who spoke Hebrew or Aramaic] because their widows were being neglected in the daily distribution" (Acts 6:1). The tensions between the two groups led to a restructuring of the community by appointing deacons to better serve their needs. This was one of the first multicultural conflicts in the young church.

Accepting and reverencing our differences without necessarily understanding them is the challenge and the heart of community life.

A Word on Conflict among Christians

Most Christians expect "good, harmonious" feelings and lots of peace in our communities as described in the Letters to the Colossians and to the Galatians. Instead, we discover conflict and tension and soon realize we are all different, and it is hard to accept that not everyone sees things "as clearly as I do!"

It is normal and healthy to experience conflict, and it is misleading to believe that conflict has no place among Christians.

Christian communities need to be open to conflict. Conflict is the uncomfortable tension of thought, feeling, or behavior that occurs whenever there are significant differences between people who interact frequently. The word "conflict" means "striking together." This striking together usually causes an uncomfortable feeling, but it is not necessarily a negative force, and it can lead to growth.

We are usually afraid of anything that is different, people who speak a different language, have a different color, view life in a different way. We do not feel comfortable allowing others to "sing their own song." We cling to our way as "the only way," or "the best way." It is normal and healthy to experience conflict, and it is misleading to believe that conflict has no place among Christians.

Jesus did not shun conflict, and he certainly challenged many of the religious institutions and practices of his time. Conflict becomes a problem only when we see ourselves in a win-or-lose situation. Christian communities can work together so that every member can be a winner and every unique process of transformation can be honored. There is richness in our diversity, and denying conflict is not necessarily the "Christian thing to do." In the midst of differences, mutual respect is always possible.

Positive Results of Conflict

- Conflict can motivate us to discover and use talents never identified before.

- Conflict invites us to be creative in discovering new ways to handle problems.

- Conflict challenges us to clarify and redefine our opinions.

- Conflict fosters spiritual and human growth and development.

- Conflict enables us to air tension and get closer to others.

Negative Results of Conflict

- Conflict can hurt deeply.

- Conflict can increase anger and frustration.

- Conflict causes stress.

- Conflict affects all areas of our life: family, work, etc.

- Conflict brings division among people.

- Conflict makes problems seem bigger.

- Conflict can lead to physical or verbal violence.

The challenge of the third millennium is to be able to respect and value one another; to see differences as gifts and all of us as a Body of many members.

The Public Face of the Christian Community

In the past few years, I have witnessed a gradual change in the way community members see their role. My early experiences of small communities were of places where people came to rest, to be with like-minded friends. As conflict began and communities realized that growth always implies change and pain, experts in group dynamics began to help us. Countless books and articles have been written on the stages of this or that. They have been extremely helpful. We have improved our understanding of group dynamics and stages of community development. But I find something missing. I have not seen much said or written about the public face of the Christian community.

Earlier in this book when I outlined the elements necessary for a community to be considered Christian, I mentioned *diakonia,* service. In the face of the challenges of our times we cannot simply care about the quality of our life together; we also need to be concerned about improving the way things are in the world around us.

> *As communities of hope, we need to believe that, while we can be agents of change, messiahs we are not.*

Our world is in need of hope. I believe that the Christian community needs to extend the hope it is giving to its members into the larger community. Beyond individual transformation and the transformation of relationships lies the promise of the transformation of society.

Just as there is conflict in the ways our individual journeys of transformation relate with one another, there will be conflict in the way our communities touch society's struggle with transformation and change. The mandate is clear, "You are the salt of the earth . . . " (Matt. 5:13). The invitation is for small communities to enter a process of discernment that will help them to achieve a balance between frozen helplessness and manic attempts to change every unjust structure in our society.

The fact that we are Christian communities invites us to look at the person in whose name we gather and serve. Jesus did what was his to do as he understood it and left many evils of his time untouched. As communities of hope, we need to believe that, while we can be agents of change, messiahs we are not.

I see hope in our journey of hope. There is a quality of relationships and care for the person and systems that only small Christian communities can offer. The invitation is how to develop that respect for one another as we journey together as one body of many members. How do we encourage members of our communities to take prophetic roles in our civic communities, in our families, in our schools, in politics?

Can a group be called a "Christian community" and remain blind to the violence, injustice, and greed that control our world today?

※

I began this book reflecting on the "challenges that emerge when two or three are gathered in Jesus' name." I hope that these pages have helped the reader to discover the intrinsic hope of the Christian life as well as the challenges that the Christian journey presents.

Today, people are lonely. We live in a culture that values competition and the urgency to be "better than...." The old song "I Did It My Way" exemplifies this attitude. In some ways this song is more American than "America the Beautiful." Society tells us that we are better and stronger when we achieve success without anyone else's help. We are influenced by consumerism; we worship heroes whose primary accomplishment has been individual success, great power, or physical strength.

What happens when I need others? What happens if I am sick or elderly or poor? What am I to expect if I become depressed and unable to cope? How will I react when the "voices" of society tell me that I have to get over it, that I can get through anything if I really want to. One of our greatest sins today is utilitarianism, and as a consequence, some people feel lonely because they are not useful.

Loneliness is the sickness of a society that fails to use symbols that reflect communal efforts rather than individual successes.

In a word, Christian life is profoundly social. It is communitarian. It happens in and to community.

Christians are no less personal persons, but they are always communal persons, never radically private persons, never autonomous individuals. Our spirituality, like our identity, emerges from relationships, of which community is a major, enduring, and necessary form.[17]

Dreaming a Christian Community

*Happy are those who dream dreams and are
ready to pay the price to make them come true.*
— Cardinal Leon Joseph Suenens

D REAMING IS AN INTEGRAL PART of living, and
dreaming implies the desire to do whatever one
can to make the dream come true. Reflecting about
Christian communities and spirituality involves a lot
of dreaming, hoping, and trusting.

Our society encourages individualism as well as
self-sufficiency. Moreover, pluralism and global consciousness can lead us to believe that in the name of
a pseudo-respect for all opinions, our society cannot
be oriented to God. To live in the spirit of community today is a big challenge, yet we are witnessing
the planet getting smaller and smaller each day, and
we know that whatever happens in Indonesia today
will affect a worker in Peru tomorrow.

Many Christians have given up the hope of changing their cities, their countries, much less the world. But thank God some of us are still dreaming. I strongly believe that without a dream and a vision we will perish.

After reflecting on Christian spirituality and community I am ready to share my dream. This is not an "impossible dream" but one of which I have seen glimpses throughout my life. The invitation is to make it sustainable for generations to come.

Someone said that things need to get really bad before they get better. I believe this is true and have seen it happen in my own lifetime, especially now. Wars, terrorism, financial chaos, global warming, climate changes, greed, genocide, violation of human rights, the rich getting richer and the poor getting poorer, families falling apart, domestic violence on the rise. As the world gets smaller and the media keeps us informed about global events even as they are happening, the temptation is to become overwhelmed and do nothing. These are the facts, and because of my faith, hope, and trust, here is my dream.

Over fifty years ago, Jesuit Pierre Teilhard de Chardin wrote:

> Someday, after mastering the winds, the waves, the tides and gravity, we shall harness for God

the energies of love, and then, for a second time in the history of the world, man will have discovered fire.

Teilhard was a dreamer. He could not be explained by ways known at that time. Some said he was a paleontologist, a scientist, while others called him a mystic. Since it was impossible to put his writings in one category, his critics observed that he was not really anything, but was just a good writer. Teilhard de Chardin was a dreamer, and dreamers cannot be boxed in a category.

When I was an adolescent and a young adult, Teilhard inspired me. His dream caught my imagination, and I began to imagine a world in which all people would harness for God the energies of love. This is still my dream, but now it is more than a dream. It has become the goal of my ministry.

I believe that a Christian community can mediate between the person and the world. The early communities, in spite of their conflicts, radiated an energy that attracted all that came in touch with them. The religious leaders asked one another, "What will we do with them? For it is obvious to all who live in Jerusalem that a notable sign has been done through them; we cannot deny it" (Acts 4:16). The situation could not have been worse. These groups were part of an early Jewish sect called the Nazareans, or the followers of the Way; they did not even have houses of worship. And yet they made a difference. I believe that we can do the same today.

I envision a community comprised of people gathered in the name of Jesus, not in their own name, Christians who value true humility, who recognize the gifts that God has given them and also the gifts that others possess, particularly those that surpass our own. I see them capable of openly collaborating with one another because they know they are the beloved of God. Without this sense of being loved by God and accepted as we are, community is not possible. One of the most common conflicts in communities is caused by competition, jealousy, and envy. Many desire to be number one or the closest friend of some person. Why? Have we forgotten how unique we are? Maybe we need to remember the words of the prophet Isaiah, "Can a woman forget her nursing-child, or show no compassion for the child of her womb? Even these may forget, yet I will not forget you. See, I have inscribed you on the palms of my hands" (49:15–16).

I dream of a community where all help each other to know and accept how beloved they are, a community where sacred space is created each time they gather in the name of Jesus. I see a community of courageous and compassionate people: Christians who can challenge unjust structures and be compassionate to their victims; communities that can foster the kind of individual and communal conversion among its members that can impact those outside.

I dream of communities that are powerful in their powerlessness, because their only power comes from God. No one tries to control another because they know the Lord in whose name they serve, the Lord who was servant to all.

In the midst of all the crises in the third millennium, we are experiencing a remarkable increase of interest in spirituality and prayer in people of all walks of life. Today's Christians live with many tensions and apparent polarities as they strive to reflect the Gospel message faithfully in their daily choices. The values of our fast-paced and impersonal society have permeated our religious institutions. Often our churches resemble successful businesses more than houses of prayer and worship. In this context, it is not surprising to find many searching for companions in their spiritual journey. The Letter to the Hebrews encouraged the early Christians to run the race with perseverance because they were "surrounded by so great a cloud of witnesses" (12:1).

I can see communities providing this kind of spiritual companionship: people on a journey helping one another to be *seers,* who can find God in the midst of everything and help their companions to do the same. I dream of communities who mediate compassion, forgiveness, and justice to the world, people who by the way they live energize others to do the same.

> *I dream of communities that are powerful in their powerlessness, because their only power comes from God.*

In the beginning God created a community, simply because God is relational and desired to share a life of intimacy with all creation. God gave us the ability to love, relate, and create freely, in God's image and likeness. We could say that God is community and that everything was created in Christ and for Christ, the Alpha and the Omega, the beginning and the end. But Christ has no body now but ours; no feet, no hands, but ours. We have been called, gifted, and sent to be Christ to our struggling world, to walk with each other in this tremendous process of transformation.

Nothing less than a total commitment to become real loving communities of believers will help the world today. It has been done before, and today it is up to the ordinary Christian in the pew, because there is no time to wait for the canonization of saints. Isn't this what John meant when he declared, "God is love"? (1 John 4:16)

> *Love alone can unite living beings so as to complete and fulfill them...for it alone joins them by what is deepest in themselves. All we need is to imagine our ability to love developing until it embraces the totality of people and the earth.*
>
> *— Pierre Teilhard de Chardin*

Notes

1. Zachary Hayes, O.F.M., "Creation," in *The New Dictionary of Catholic Spirituality* (Collegeville, Minn.: Liturgical Press, 1993), 242.

2. See Jim Forest, "Dorothy Day, Saint and Trouble-maker," lecture originally given on October 10, 1997, at Marquette University, Milwaukee, published in *Guadalupe,* the newsletter of Casa Maria, the Catholic Worker house in Tucson.

3. Kenneth R. Overberg, S.J., "The Incarnation: Why God Wanted to Become Human," in *Catholic Update* (St. Anthony Messenger Press), December 2002.

4. Seamus Mulholland, O.F.M., "Incarnation in Franciscan Spirituality," *Franciscan* (January 2001).

5. St. Irenaeus, cited in *Catechism of the Catholic Church* (St. Louis: Ligouri Publications, 1994), no. 460.

6. St. Athanasius, cited in ibid.

7. Bernard J. Lee, S.M., "Community," in *The New Dictionary of Catholic Spirituality* (Collegeville, Minn.: Liturgical Press, 1993), 184.

8. Ibid., 187.

9. Philip Sheldrake, *Spirituality and History* (New York: Crossroad, 1992), 58.

10. Ibid., 33.

11. *Catechism of the Catholic Church*, no. 2709.

12. Francis L. Gross Jr. and Toni Perior Gross, *The Making of a Mystic: Seasons in the Life of Teresa of Avila* (Albany: State University of New York Press, 1993), 206.

13. *Summa Theologica* III, 82. 2 ad 3; cf. 82. 9 ad 2.

14. Adrian Fortescue, "Liturgy," *Catholic Encyclopedia,* vol. 9. (New York: Robert Appleton Company, 1910), *www.newadvent.org/cathen/09306a.htm.*

15. Henri J. M. Nouwen, *Life of the Beloved* (New York: Crossroad, 1997), 26.

16. The Spiritual Exercises of St. Ignatius of Loyola are a month-long program of meditations, prayers, considerations, and contemplative practices. They are designed to help a retreatant (usually with the aid of a spiritual director) to experience a deeper conversion into life with God in Christ, to allow our personal stories to be interpreted by being subsumed in a Story of God.

17. Bernard J. Lee, S.M., "Community," *The New Dictionary of Catholic Spirituality* (Collegeville, Minn.: Liturgical Press, 1993), 191.

"Truly a spirituality for the 21st century!"
—*Dolores Leckey*

Catholic Spirituality for Adults

General Editor
Michael Leach

Forthcoming volumes include:

- *Following Jesus* by John Shea

To learn more about forthcoming titles in the series, go to *orbisbooks.com.*

For free study guides and discussion ideas on this book, go to *www.rclbenziger.com.*

Please support your local bookstore.

Thank you for reading *The Spirituality of Community* by Adele Gonzalez. We hope you found it beneficial.